BOUND FOR GLORY

BOUND FOR GLORY

A Practical Handbook for Raising a Victorious Family

R. C. SPROUL JR.

TOLLE LEGE PRESS

Bound for Glory

Copyright © 2003, 2008 by R.C. Sproul Jr.
Published by **Tolle Lege Press**
      P.O. Box 5069
      White Hall, WV 26555

First Printing: 2003
Second Printing: February 2008
Third Printing: February 2013

Cover design: Adam Stiles and Joseph Darnell

Printed in the United States of America.

Sproul, R. C. (Robert Craig), 1965–
    Bound for Glory: A practical handbook for raising a
        victorious family / R. C. Sproul Jr.

   ISBN-10: 0-9754846-5-6

To Denise,
my covenant woman

CONTENTS

FOREWORD

R.C. SPROUL SR.

Where are you bound? When I use the word "bound" in this question, I'm not talking about being in a state whereby someone has bound your hands and feet with chains or a rope. Rather I'm using the term "bound" with respect to a destination. When we're bound for something, it means that we have directed our movement to a certain place we hope to finish.

We live in a culture that has cut us off from our ultimate destination. The mantra of the humanist and of the naturalist is this: We have come from nothing, and we are bound for nothing. We are told that as human beings, we are the result of the chance collision of atoms, that we have emerged gratuitously from the slime. We are at best cosmic accidents. Our origin is insignificant, and our destiny is equally insignificant. We've come from the dust, and we will return to the dust, and human life is a tiny blip between those two points of origin and destination.

The folly of the humanist is that he says our origin is meaningless and our destiny is meaningless, but in between these two poles, life is meaningful, and humans have dignity. If ever there was a philosophy built upon wish projection, this is the one. If indeed our origin is meaningless and our destiny is meaningless, it would be impossible to have any significant meaning in between.

Over against this pessimistic view of humanity is the Biblical view that teaches us that our origin is found in the purposive act of God's divine creation. And though we come from the dust, that dust is molded by the Creator, and the Creator breathes into that dust so that we become living beings, beings that are made in God's own image. The purpose of the act of creation is not ultimate ruin, but rather what God creates, He works to redeem. The destination of the Christian is not the abyss of meaninglessness. The destination of the Christian is heaven. In so far as our final destiny is heaven, our final destiny is also glorious. We start as dust. We end in glory. The title of this book by R.C. Sproul Jr. embraces the truth of that Biblical affirmation, that as Christians we are bound for glory. The implications of that final point of destiny are massive with respect to how we get there and what we are to do between our origin and our destiny. The goal of parenting is to ground our children, indeed our whole family, in the truths that God delivers to prepare us for life in eternity. If we are bound for glory, we are to travel a road that will get us there. And though that road may be marred by pitfalls and potholes, nevertheless the guide that Scripture gives us is one that steers us around the potholes and to our ultimate destination. This book teaches people how to steer their families and their children to the destination God has appointed for His people. It is a roadmap to gloryland.

I confess that my son has been far more diligent in training his family in the things of God than I was in mine. His diligence and devotion in these matters have far exceeded anything I have ever dreamed of. I am delighted to write this foreword that you may go forward to learn how to reach the destination of glory.

Thanksgiving, 2007
Orlando
Dr. R.C. Sproul Sr.

INTRODUCTION

Different books take different journeys to get into print. The book you are holding began as a radio program and as a video series produced by my father's ministry, Ligonier Ministries. That series included not only a series of talks by me on the subject of the family, but also a series of talks by a family, conversations about the family between my father and me. One such conversation preceded the taping, and another came after. I think it important to include these conversations in the book, not only for what is taught *in* the conversation, but for what is taught *by* the conversation. What I hope will come through is something that you never grow out of—the call to honor your parents.

A Father and Son Conversation

R.C. Sproul, Senior: Over thirty years ago, when I was working at a church in Cincinnati, I became close friends with a man who was a detective on the Cincinnati police force, and one of the things that was exciting to discover in my friendship with him was that he had become a Christian as a result of the direct influence of his son and his daughter. Both of his kids became Christians before he did and as a result of their testimony in the home he came to Christ.

While I can't say that I became a Christian because of the influence of my children on my life, I do relate to my friend's experience back in Cincinnati in that I have been profoundly influenced and instructed on some very significant things about the Christian faith from my own children, and certainly not the least of which is the influence I've had from my son, Dr. R.C. Sproul, the handsome, particularly with respect to the covenant family.

When Ligonier decided to put together a teaching series on the family, one of the questions that came to me was, Should I do that lecture series? and I said, "Well I could, if we want to have Ligonier's second-best do it," because I really believe that R.C. Jr. knows so much more about this subject than I do and I thought it would be much more fitting to have him do it. I mean we know how biased parents can be and so on, but in all honesty I have never met anybody in my life who has displayed to me a commitment to training up their children in the things of God like R.C Jr. has; and I have witnessed what he does with my grandchildren, which absolutely amazes me on the one hand and shames me on the other. I remember when R.C. was a little boy, and his older sister, that I prayed for them constantly and knew the biblical passage that nobody has any greater joy than to see their children walking in the Lord. And it was my great desire to see them grow up in the nurture and admonition of the Lord, and we'll talk a little bit about our experiences in our home, but we didn't come anywhere close to the discipline of training children as he has developed in his family, and he has shown me so many things that I wanted to let everybody else have that opportunity.

But one other thing I want to say is that I've been listening on the radio in the afternoon to my friend Alistair Begg, who has given a series of lectures, and one of the lectures that he gave was on the Hebrew *shema*. We're all familiar with—at least those of us who have Jewish friends—that they may have that little scroll on their doorpost that contains the words of the *shema*: "Hear O Israel, the Lord our God is one, and you must love the Lord your God with all of your heart and all your mind and soul and strength." And then it goes on to give the mandate that God gives to the parents in Israel to speak of these things with their children when they rise up on the morning, when they go to bed at night, and in all the circumstances that the children may be taught by the parents. And the tendency in our culture is to transfer the responsibility of training in godliness to the Christian school or to the church, to the Sunday school, rather than seeing this as a mandate given to the parents by the Lord Himself. And so, R.C, I'm just so glad that you are willing to do this series on the covenant family, and sort of to frame that, I'd like you to talk to me a little bit today about some of your experiences and our experiences as family. I think that might be of interest to people.

R.C. Sproul, Junior: Well I think so too, and I think that you were too hard on yourself. Everything that I want to be—I have a danger in my life that my job as a man is to come to the Scripture and say, "What does the Scripture say I'm supposed to do as a man?" My temptation is to look to you and say to myself, "I love my father. My father's my hero. That's what I want to be."

Senior: It is a sad thing. I understand. I can feel your pain there. I've been trying to get him to say that for thirty-five years, you know...

Junior: I don't know. It might take another thirty-five years for me to continue.

Senior: Let me ask you a question, all right? When do you become a man?

Junior: When you say I'm a man.

Senior: When I say you're a man, okay. Good.

Junior: And as I'm listening to you, I'm thinking about, of course, my own desire to be a godly husband and father and to make you proud. Before I came down here I spoke with my children, and I said, "Daddy's got to go do some work. Daddy's going to go and speak about the Christian family." And I said, "I want you to know why. The reason Daddy's going down to talk about the Christian family is because people know you." I said, "Your grandfather knows you, and your grandfather is so pleased with you that he thinks I can come talk to people about the family." I said, you know the Scripture says—and they know this from when we studied together through Proverbs that children can and should, be a delight to their parents—that they bring honor to their parents." I said,

"Daddy has the honor because of you guys." I want to return the children to the Lord, to whom they belong and say, "These are yours, and I'm dependent upon you," and in a similar way I return them to my father. One of the things we're going to talk about in this series is one of the things that we're missing. As Christians we look out in the world, and the world has got the family falling apart, and our vision is to defend the family and our understanding of the family, because the world is so confused on the issue. But it's so narrow that what we need to do is get beyond the vision of the nuclear family and get back to a vision of patriarchy.

This past weekend I was speaking at a conference put on by a fellow who publishes a magazine called *Patriarch* and I talked about this there as well. I want to be a faithful member of the Sproul clan, and you are the patriarch. My eldest is nine, but even though she's only nine I'm telling all of my children, "Look, there's going to come a day when you're going to be the heads of your homes." I tell my daughter, "You're going to have a husband, God willing," and my son, "You're going to have a wife, God-willing, and you're going to have to be ready to lead your families." And so it's a wonderful experience to be able to teach them. As you know, we homeschool our children, and the last few weeks Denise and I have been working out schedules and what are we going to cover and when are we going to do it, and we've decided that twice a week I'm going to meet with my son and do Bible study with him. And when he found that out, his face lit up and his eyes turned to saucers. That whole week he was telling me, "Four more days, Daddy. Three more days, Daddy." And we sat down, and I began to talk about what does it mean to be the head of your home and began to talk to him about what I want him to do. I said, " You already have a realm over which you rule." One of his jobs is to feed the cats and the dogs and the chickens.

Senior: Oh my, you've entrusted those famous chickens to Campbell.

Junior: Yes, and that was a mistake.

Senior: Oh, I don't know. I would think that they'd be faring as well as they were before.

Junior: But that's the point. Won't I be embarrassed when he succeeds where I have failed. There is no place to go but up. He can't do any worse than I did. He does that and he cleans the baseboards in the house. And I explained to him, "You know Daddy has given Mommy the responsibility and the authority to keep the house tidy and neat because you know what would happen if I did that, and she has now delegated to you the responsibility of the baseboards, and that's what I want you to do. This is a practice for you to rule. This is your area of responsibility, and I want to see you do a good job."

You know, this is part of what we mean about talking with our children when we rise up and when we lie down. My son has a chore to clean the baseboards in the house, and I want to turn that into a lesson on what it means to be a godly man. And that kind of thing is in many ways—you don't think so—but in many ways something that I learned from you. I mean we were not homeschooled. I wish we had been, but in God's providence we weren't. But out of anybody who wasn't home schooled I doubt there were many parents who were more involved than you were and who also, outside of the raw academics, took the time to teach the lessons.

Senior: Well you know, R.C., you talk about the patriarchal thing, and I have to say to you, I mean when you get choked up about looking to your father and so on, one of the greatest pains of my life is that you never met your grandfather—who was my greatest hero. There was no one in the world that I wanted to please more than I wanted to please him. And he died when I was seventeen years old, long, of course, before you were born. And so you've never had the opportunity to meet him.

Junior: Right.

Senior: But also you never had the opportunity to meet my grandfather, for whom we were both named. His name was R.C. He was known as R.C., and he really was, in my experience, the patriarch. I never think of myself as being a patriarch. When I think of patriarchy in our family, I think of the one they called R.C.—my grandfather. He was such a godly gentleman, and "gentleman" was the word that really captured him. He died when I was six years old, and so you would think that I wouldn't have many memories of my grandfather, but I have. I'm filled with memories of him. There was a life-long impact on me that came from that man, from his model. I mean I spent every Sunday afternoon with him from the time I was born until the time I was six years old, and in that small window of opportunity, he made an enormous impact on me. And then after he died, the impact that my father had also—

there was a sense in which I could see through my father to his father.

Junior: I understand that.

Senior: Do you?

Junior: Yes, I do.

Senior: Don't you sort of feel like you maybe know my father a little bit, even though you never met him?

Junior: Yes. In fact, as I was preparing for this particular series I was thinking just exactly that thing. I was thinking, "You know, I never met my grandfather, but I know that he was a great man of God," and I know it because of what you say about him, how you feel about him, and I know that you wouldn't have that deep and abiding love and respect for him if he weren't.

Senior: But not just my father and grandfather and everything, but as a boy growing up on my father's side of the cousins and everything I was the youngest one. So I had all these older cousins.

Junior: You were precious.

Senior: Yeah, I was the precious one. I was the baby of the family, and our family was the kind that every Thanksgiving, every Christmas, every Easter, the whole family—because they all lived in the Pittsburgh area—the whole family gathered together for the day. And I also lived in an extended family. Growing up we had my father, my mother, my sister, and I, plus an uncle, an aunt, and their daughter, another uncle, another cousin, plus my grandmother all living under the same roof. We had twelve rooms in our house by the time my dad stopped adding on to accommodate all these family members that we had growing up. So you talk about an extended family, and I was the youngest, of course. But I was overwhelmed by all these people, and they were my favorite people in the world. My favorite days were those days of Easter and Thanksgiving and Christmas when the whole family got together. And to this day, those people who still are left are the most important people in my life, and when it comes right down to it, you can have friends, and you can have acquaintances and buddies, co-laborers and all that. As close as those relationships and as meaningful as they are, to me there's just nothing like family and yet I talk to people all the time who are from so-called "broken" homes, "broken" families who don't have that sense of strong familial ties. What a terrible, terrible tragedy it is to have families that don't have the kind of bonding that I experienced. I look back at my home life, and I think I was extremely blessed. I was never abused. I was encouraged, I was disciplined, I was loved, and not just by my mother and father but by my aunt who lived with me. I called her my step-mother-aunt, and when she died it was like having my mother die. And my cousin who for ten years lived in our house, is ten years older than I am. She's not my cousin, she's my sister as far as I'm concerned. And it's a wonderful experience.

Junior: Well it is, and it's a shaping experience as you've just described. And the thing about one of our weaknesses in our families is we think that if we all live under the same roof then that's the same thing, but it takes time and it takes intentionality, to build those bonds. And we miss that because we all have our separate lives.

Senior: Well R.C., I know that you know that your mother loves you and that your father loves you and that your wife loves you and your children love you and all of that, but I'll tell you what. One of the things that I notice is that because you live in Virginia and your sister still lives in my house (she has for twenty years with her husband and their kids), your sister's crazy about you.

Junior: I know.

Senior: She really is. I mean she's always worried about, "What's R.C. doing? What can we do for him," and all of that. She's nuts about you.

Junior: Well maybe she's afraid for me. "What's R.C. doing?" may actually mean, "What in the world does he think he's doing?" It is a great thing, and one of the great things about the fact that she is here is that when I get to be here, I get to be with her as well. When you all come up together to visit in Virginia it's a great thing. And it's hard for me when I speak to my children and say, "Okay, we're going to go see..." and I have to go through everybody instead of just saying "your grandparents." It's the family coming back together, and it's a wonderful thing.

Senior: Well R.C., I'm just a little excited that you're here and that we're going to have this series on the family because I would like to have other people benefit the way I have from what you've learned and that what you're talking about this week is not abstract theory.

Junior: No.

Senior: This thing has real shoe leather to it. You're walking the walk, not just talking the talk and I'm looking forward with really joyful anticipation to this series and I want to thank you for coming to do it.

Junior: It's my pleasure.

Chapter One:
The Family Plan

My father and I have several things in common. One such thing is that we are often asked difficult questions. The question he is asked more than any other is, "Where did evil come from?" The question I am asked more than any other is, "What's it like to have R.C. Sproul as your father?" His difficulty is theological, mine is historical. That is, I don't know how to answer my question, because I have nothing with which to compare it. It's not as though I spent fifteen years as Michael Jordan's son, and now I'm R.C. Sproul's son.

I can tell you, however, two aspects of being his son that are probably unusual. Many times, when I meet young men, I face the challenge of the gunslinger. They know that they will probably never have a theological shootout with my father, so they settle for me. They delight to try to stump me, though when they succeed, victory can be rather hollow. After all, it's not like they gunned down the real R.C. Sproul. Women, on the other hand, don't want to shoot me, they want to comfort me. They tend to be sensitive to the slings and arrows that come with being the son of....

There is, also, to borrow a phrase, a *tertium quid*, a third option. Sometimes people meet me, get this puzzled look on their face, and note, "You sure don't look like your father." Then I point out where the family resemblance lies, in our mutual magnificent middles. We both have bellies to beat the band. There are a host of other similarities as well. We both write books. We both, from time to time, are on the radio. We both serve as pastors of churches. We are both Presbyterians. Oh, and we share a name as well.

Both of us likewise have great wives. I have outstanding children, while my poor father has only one, my sister. We do, in some sense, a similar kind of work, in the same way that a paper airplane and the Space Shuttle do similar kinds of things. We also believe essentially the same things. What you get with me then, is an approximation of what he thinks, but lacking his depth of wisdom, and skill of delivery.

There are, however, some significant differences between us as well. We come from different worlds. My father remembers World War II. I barely remember the soldiers coming home from Vietnam. My father went through his teens when everyone liked Ike. When I was that age Ronald Reagan occupied the White House. And for all our similarities, I'm sure the bean counters at Visa are able to tell us apart. He, I'm sure, gets rather more leeway in his credit than I'll ever get.

But there is an important difference as well in the way we were raised. Yes, we both grew up in western Pennsylvania. But my father, when he grew up, lived not only with his mother, his father, and his sister, but an uncle and aunt, a cousin, several other relations and someone who wasn't even blood-related. When I was a boy there was just my mother, my father and my sister. In my own house now, there are probably more people than were in his house, but they still are only my immediate family. We have no aunts or uncles, but we have been blessed with six children, so far.

Not only, however, was his extended family in my father's home when he grew up, but the rest of the extended family were also nearby. The Sprouls occupied several of the hills around Pittsburgh, and often gathered the whole clan together to feast. I, on the other hand, live amidst the hills of western Virginia and my parents are over seven hundred miles away. My children's cousins are likewise hours and hours away by car. While there may be reasons for this separation, it remains a sad thing. We lack a closeness as families, at least geographically.

What causes that? There is a battle—a critical front on the broader culture war—over the nature of the family. One of the weapons you need to fight a culture war is words. You want to have the good words on your side, if at all possible, and *family* is one of the best words. Everybody, after all, is in favor of families. If you can associate your agenda with "family" you will make headway in selling that agenda. Thus we have political campaigns being won or lost based on who succeeds in being perceived as for "family values." Now what is a family value? The only thing I know has precious little to do with politics. I am pro-family values because with six children, when I go to the grocery store, I don't buy the large box, I don't buy the jumbo box, I buy the "family value" sized box of laundry detergent. But I don't suppose that any political party wants to be known as those who are in favor of big boxes of detergent. Even those who might have a tough row to hoe to claim the "family values" mantle have found a way to seize the word. You may have seen the bumper sticker that says, "Hate is not a family value." Here those on the left can seize "family" while pinning "hate," one of the bad words, on those on the right.

There is then, a great battle being waged over how we define the family, that is directly related to the battle for the survival of the family. Why would the enemies of God be intent on destroying the family? Because the family is one of precious few institutions established by God. The devil wants to destroy the family because the family matters. The sad news is that as the church joins this battle, we have joined it so late, and we're so far behind, that we are fighting what strategists call a rear-guard action. We're retreating, while trying to save what we can. The typical vision of the family in the church, in fact, is so anemic that we think we're doing well if we can keep a husband and wife together, while they raise a child or two. We think if we succeed in doing this, that we ought to win a trophy. Only a generation or two ago, however, such a family would be looked upon with sadness as an almost family, as a portion of a family. Back then when people thought of family, they thought of homes like the one in which my father was raised. A generation ago when people thought of families they thought in terms of patriarchs and matriarchs. They had a multigenerational view, whereas we're doing all we can simply to save the nuclear family.

Worse still, even when our families manage to stay together, we manage to tear them apart. The culture is content to let a husband, a wife and one or two children share a roof, as long as it can ensure that they do not share a life. There need not be any divorce, any broken homes, in order to tear asunder a family. It happens within our homes. Popular culture looks at our families not as families but as a collection of individuals in disjointed demographic groups. Often even the designs of our homes reflect that shift in thinking. Too many homes are nothing other than apartment complexes, wherein each member of the "family" is given their own little space, complete with their own bathroom, their own television, their own Xbox. If we ever do get together it's usually at the mess-hall, and that is getting rarer every year. But even when we are all together under the same roof, we are still divided. Each demographic group has its own diversions to fill the time. Dad may have his nose buried in *Sports Illustrated*, while Mom is reading *Redbook*, or worse still, *Cosmopolitan*. Up in her room, Princess is reading *Seventeen* magazine, while Junior is sitting in front of the television flipping through *Boy's Life*. We may think, if we don't look beneath the surface, "What a lovely family." But the truth is that this is a family already separated. If we could even get them together in the room, it would only be to watch the blue-eyed glowing idol in their living room.

But it gets worse. We have much the same problem in the church. Just about the only time a typical family is together when it comes to time at church is when they are riding there in the car. We have a plethora of programs, always age, and sometimes gender, segregated. Mom goes off to her Women in the Church or Awana circle. Dad heads off to his Promise Keepers meeting. Princess is at her youth group meeting, while Junior is watching animated vegetable videos in the children's church. We enter the house of God together, only to scatter in different directions. Even within the church we're being torn apart.

We learned this, as we so often do, from the culture around us. The rest of the week follows the same pattern. Come Monday, Mom is off to her work and Dad to his, while Princess spends her day at the middle school and Junior at the grade school. Everything about our modern culture pushes us away from each other. Each demographic group has its own language, its own musical styles. Go to the mall sometime, what I call the temple of consumption. There you will find as many as a half-dozen different sections of women's clothes, for a half-dozen different ages. The generation gap no longer exists simply between teenagers and their parents, but between teenagers and twenty-somethings, and tweenagers, *ad nauseum*.

We seem to think that if we can keep all this separateness together under one roof that we are doing okay. The truth is we are failing miserably, even when we think we are succeeding. We're allowing our families to be torn apart, because we are allowing our families to be molded by the wisdom of this world.

God, in His mercy and power, has established in this world four institutions. One is the individual. The second is the family. After that comes the church and finally, He has also established the state. The drive in our age is to reduce that number down to two, to eliminate what the sociologists call the "mediating institutions," the family and the church. The culture looks at each of us principally as individuals who are likewise a part of the state. Our identity in the family or the church is coincidental, if not problematic. The family and the church are mediating, or middle, institutions, in that they protect us from being swallowed into one of the other two institutions. In this battle, the world encourages us to think of our loyalties only in terms of to ourselves as individuals, or to the state. If a third loyalty is permitted, it is merely to our own demographic group. We tend then to think of ourselves by ourselves. We lack a family identity. We have no notion of being part of something bigger than ourselves. We are individualists, rather than family-ists.

How do we overcome this? What we find when we come to the Word of God for our answers is this: we are kept together, we are bound together, we are a unity as families and as the church of Jesus Christ by and through the Biblical understanding of the *covenant*. Covenant is one of those words and concepts that pop up over and over again in the Bible. It is central to our convictions, and should be central to how we understand the Bible. But it also needs to be central to our understanding of the family.

The relationship between the covenant and the family really hit home on a rather odd occasion. It happened when I was being ordained to the ministry. In most Presbyterian denominations, the process of becoming a minister of the gospel is something of an ordeal. We even refer to this time as our "ordination trials." First, you have to preach a sermon to a group of pastors and lay leaders in the denomination. Then, you must take an exam. But when all that is done you have to "stand on the floor of presbytery." This means that those same men who listened to you preach with a careful ear, are now free to ask you questions. They can ask personal questions or theological questions, biblical questions or historical questions. My job, standing alone in front of all these godly men, is to answer the questions. Their goal in asking the questions is at least two-fold. First, they want to make sure I know my stuff. Second, they want to make sure I don't believe anything completely off the wall. And third, I think, they want to see how eager I am to be ordained, if I'm willing to suffer through this ordeal.

Sometimes they'll ask something easy like, "Tell us about how you came to know the Lord." Other times they'll ask for an outline of the book of Zephaniah. Or they might say, "Please tell us a little about the great chain of salvation in Romans 8." (Or they might fail to remind me that it's found in the eighth chapter of Romans.) During my trials I was asked this question, "Would you please list for us, Mr. Sproul, the covenants that God made with man?" "Yes," I started, because you'd better always start with yes, "God made covenant with Adam. Then there was His covenant with Noah. Next was the Abrahamic covenant. He made covenant with David, and with Jesus."

The room in which I stood was not filled exclusively with godly men. There was also there at least one godly woman, my own dear wife. After the whole ordeal was over, as we were driving back home she told me that as I was answering the question on the covenants, one gentleman leaned over to another and said, "He forgot the covenant with Abraham." I said, "Isn't that interesting? Either that gentleman didn't hear me say "...the Abrahamic covenant..." or he didn't know that "Abrahamic" is the adjectival form meaning, "of or pertaining to Abraham." But as we were having this conversation, a thought entered my mind. "You know dear," I went on, "there actually was no covenant in the Bible with Abraham." She, of course, must have thought that my ordeal had caused me to flip my lid. "There was in fact," I went on, "no covenant with Adam, nor one with Noah, nor one with David. You see, every time God makes a covenant in the Bible, He always makes it "with you and your seed."

God makes covenants with families, and in so doing, He binds us together. Covenants, in fact, are what define us as families. We are, as families, a group of people in covenant with God. We are unified by and for His covenant. But there is yet another level to the covenant and the family. Not only are we in covenant with God, we are likewise in covenant with each other. That is how I define the family, a series of horizontal covenants among men that is, as a whole, in vertical covenant with God.

The horizontal covenants include, of course, the covenant between a husband and a wife, the covenant between a wife and a husband (this is what we are doing when making marriage vows—covenanting together) and the covenant between parents and children.

We haven't made much headway in defining the family, however, if we don't yet know what a covenant is. We may have some idea, but just as with the family, too often our understanding of the covenant has been distorted by the wisdom of the world. For instance, we tend to think of covenant as a rather pious and archaic word for contract. Contracts we understand. We deal with them all the time. We have contracts with our employers, contracts with our cell phone companies, and some of us even have contracts with our book publishers. And there is a connection between covenants and contracts. When you have a contract you have two parties who come together in an agreement. One party promises to do one thing, the other party promises to do another. Tolle Lege Press, for example, has promised to try to persuade people to buy this book, and to pay me a percentage of each sale. I, on the other hand, have promised to create this book, and to deliver it by a particular date.

But there is yet another similarity. Contracts often have penalties as well. If, for instance, Tolle Lege fails to publish this book, they might have to pay a penalty. If I fail to meet my deadline, I might have to pay a penalty. Covenants, likewise, include commitments by the parties involved to perform some act or another. And they likewise include sanctions for failure to meet the terms of the agreement. So, in one sense, covenants are very much like contracts.

The differences, however, are critical. Contracts are something over which there are negotiations. The two parties come to the negotiating table, and see if they can hammer out an agreement. Suppose Tolle Lege had offered me all the brussels sprouts I could eat, in exchange for this book. Would I have to take this deal? Of course not. Or suppose that I sent Tolle Lege a manuscript that consisted of hundreds of pages with "Families are good" repeated over and over. Would they have an obligation to publish the book? By no means. Either party can walk away from the negotiations before there is agreement.

Understand that when God came to Abraham and said: "Abraham, have I got a deal for you. I am going to give you a son. I'm going to give you a land. I'm going to bring nations from you. I'm going to bless the nations through you. But wait, there's more; I also will be your God," Abraham was not free to reply: "That's a great opening offer Lord. Throw in thirty wives and you have a deal." God wouldn't counter-offer, "I'll give you ten wives, but you'll have to give up on the land." There is no back and forth when God makes covenant with man. When God speaks, that settles the matter. But sadly, we look for a contract when God has given a covenant. "God, I'll do this, and I'll do that. I'll obey this law, and that law, but this other one, you know the one, we're going to have to have some serious talks about it."

In like manner, we allow the world to define what the family is and what it is called to be. We think we can remake the family in any manner we wish. But the horizontal covenants are determined by the vertical covenant. God decides how things will work. Because not only are the covenants with God not something we can negotiate over, they are also not something we can refuse. That is, God didn't say, "Here's the deal. You can take it or leave it. Rather He says, "Here's the deal." We can't escape the authority of God, no matter how much the world tells us we can. In fact, the very essence of the family covenant is that we cannot escape it.

The verse in the Old Testament that was most central to the heart of the children of Israel, the passage that defined them as a people is known as the *shema*: "Hear, O Israel, the Lord your God, the Lord is one" (Deut. 6:4). What follows is the great commandment: "And you shall love the Lord your God with all your heart, mind, soul and strength" (Deut. 6:5). And what follows that? Over and over for the rest of this most sacred chapter God commands, "Tell your children, tell your children, tell your children. Tell them who I am. Tell them what I have done. Tell them what I require. Teach them my covenants."

My prayer is that through this book we might develop a more covenantal, a more biblical understanding of the family. I pray we will catch that ancient vision, that we will strive to keep covenant in our families, for our families and as families. I pray that we will be equipped to put back together, by God's covenantal grace, what the world has torn asunder, the family. We can pray such with confidence, because we serve a God who is not only Lord of the covenant, but is also our loving Father. And He never has and never will break covenant, no matter what the cost.

CHAPTER TWO:

THE FAMILY'S CHIEF END

We noted in the last chapter that there is a great war being fought in our culture over the nature of the family. There are principalities and powers among us who would delight for us to have a confused and distorted understanding of what the family is. If we belong to Christ, however, we know that our understanding of the family needs to come not from the world, but from the Word of God. Only the Bible can rightly tell us what the family is.

Our tendency in the church, I'm afraid, is to mix together the Bible's understanding of the family with the world's understanding of the family. We perform too narrow a reformation in our thinking. When the world shows us Heather and her two mommies, we rightly react against it. But we fail to see clearly, and fully, what is wrong with this picture. If we want to understand the nature of the family in a biblical way, we need not only to understand what are its constituent parts, but what is its goal or purpose. In which direction, toward what end, are we to be leading our families? The best place to find that answer is to go back to the beginning, to find out where the family came from. To do that, we need to turn to the second chapter of Genesis.

Most of us are somewhat familiar with the content of Genesis 2. We know that there Moses records similar things to what he recorded in the first chapter of Genesis. In both places, under the inspiration of the Holy Spirit, without error, Moses tells us how God created the world. He tells us what God did the first day, and the second, and so on. My children, when they took their very first history test, went to the beginning. We asked them, "What did God do on day one? What did God do on day two?" They passed with flying colors.

Because there is a battle over this portion of the Bible in the culture, and because so many people refuse to believe God on the issue of creation, we too often tend to look at these chapters as mere fodder for the battle. And in so doing we miss some important themes. God did not inspire Moses to write these words principally so that two thousand years later we would know how to answer the Darwinists. We often miss how He ended His day. We are told several times, "And God saw that it was good." God pronounces His divine benediction, or His good word on His own creative work. He assesses what He has done, and announces that He is pleased with His work. God is here speaking prophetically, pronouncing a judgment of weal upon the creation. No doubt, had we been there, we would have concurred.

Of course, for us there is a bit of dramatic irony going on. Though Moses has made no mention of it yet, we are well aware that there is yet in the background something rather sinister. The serpent, we know, is coming soon. So while we're hearing, "And it was good... and it was good...and it was good," in the background we hear some scary mood music. What's interesting, however, is that God doesn't wait until the serpent steps onto the scene to pronounce His first malediction. God declared that there was something "not good" long before the serpent first slithered in. Moses tells us in Genesis 2:18: "And the Lord God said, 'It is not good that man should be alone.'"

Our tendency with this passage is to stop right here. If we were to peruse all the books on the family purporting to be written from a Christian perspective, I suspect we would find that most, if not all of them would come to this passage, just as I have done. That it is not good that man should be alone, and that God so decreed it, ought to let us know how important marriage and family is. And it does tell us that. But this passage also tells us so much more.

We have to ask, "Why is it not good that man should be alone?" These same "Christian" books will posit their own theories. "Oh," they might say, "it is not good because men are from Mars and women are from Venus. God knew that they would need each other to balance the other one out." Or they might reason, "Poor Adam there in the garden all alone. What he needed was companionship. We are, after all, social creatures. So God made Eve to keep Adam company. Companionship is the point of the family, it's what marriage is all about." We agree with God. It is a problem that man is alone. But then we leave God behind as we try to figure out what the problem is.

Adam, you will remember, had made no complaint. God didn't declare His divine displeasure after Adam came and whined that he was lonely. It wasn't his idea; Adam didn't say, "God, it is not good that I am alone." The answer as to why it was not good—the revelation of the problem—is found in the answer God gives in the rest of the passage. "And the Lord God said, 'It is not good that man should be alone. I will make him a helper comparable to him.'" The problem is clear enough: Adam didn't need a soul-mate. He didn't need a boon to his self-esteem. He didn't need a balance. What Adam did need was help. He was incapable on his own.

I understand why I need help. I am reminded of my insufficiency daily. But why should Adam need help? Is it because the ground stubbornly refuses to be fruitful? Of course not. Adam is in paradise. And he's not planning on leaving on a trip. God did not say, "Adam needs a helper because he's going to get lost. Because he's a man, he won't stop and ask for directions, so I'll make him a woman to tell him where to go." You can't look at this picture of Adam in the garden and argue that something's missing here in paradise. If we want to know why Adam needs help, we need to go further back, into Genesis 1:

> Then God said, "Let us make man in our image according to our likeness. Let them have dominion over the fish of the sea, over the birds of the air, and over the cattle, over all the earth, and over every creeping thing that creeps on the earth." So, God created man in His own image. In the image of God He created him.

Male and female, He created them. Then, God blessed them and said to them, "Be fruitful and multiply. Fill the earth and subdue it. Have dominion over the fish of the sea, over the birds of the air, and over every living thing that moves on the earth" (Gen. 1:26- 28).

It is here that we find God's charge to Adam, God's covenant with Adam. It was not good that man should be alone as he set about the business of exercising dominion over the creation.

The *creation* or *dominion mandate*, of course, was given in the context of the garden. Adam and Eve were yet without sin. The ground would cooperate with their labors, and bear much fruit. But then the serpent makes his appearance, and all the joy of the creation comes crashing down in the fall. Adam and Eve are no longer what they once were. They are at enmity with God, separated from Him. Now they, and all who would flow from them, are spiritually dead. So now what does God have in store for them?

While Adam and Eve could, and did change, God Himself does not and cannot change. And neither does the covenant. Neither does the dominion mandate. Consider the curses that God pronounces in the aftermath of the fall. Adam is not fired from his job. He is not told, "You shall no longer rule over the creation." Instead he is told that the creation will be more stingy in its obedience. Eve is not told that she will no longer be fruitful and multiply. Rather, she is told that when she gives birth, it will be with great pain. Although they are expelled from the garden, the command still abides.

The Scripture then recounts a brief overview of ancient history, tracing the line of Seth and the line of Cain, side by side. Eventually the two sides become indistinguishable as the power of sin grows over the creation. God, in His just wrath, sends the flood to wipe out every living thing, save for Noah and his wife, their three sons and their wives, and all the animals on the ark. God in His grace dries up the water, and as Noah leaves the ark God speaks His law once more: "So God blessed Noah and his sons, and said to them: 'Be fruitful and multiply, and fill the earth'" (Gen. 9:1). It is the same command. The dominion mandate abides. It does not change.

It still hasn't changed to this day, except in one important way. When the original command was given it was in paradise. Now, not only do we have ground that produces thorns and thistles, not only do we no longer have peace among the animals, not only does child-birth bring with it great pain, but the dominion mandate must now be done in the context of perpetual warfare. The job remains, but instead of exercising dominion in a context of peace—with God's blessing—warfare now surrounds us.

After Adam and Eve fall into sin, God comes to visit them in the garden. He asks why they are hiding, and they expose their sin by confessing their nakedness. God asks if they have eaten the fruit, and the blame game begins. Eve blames the serpent. Adam first blames Eve, "It was the woman" and then—in a backward kind of way—God Himself, "that You gavest me." Since we've already looked briefly at God's curse on Adam and Eve, we know that hope abides because they yet have their task before them. But the great news comes in the context of the curse which is pronounced upon the serpent:

> So, the Lord God said to the serpent, "Because you have done this, you are more cursed than all the cattle and more than every beast of the field. On your belly you shall go, and you shall eat dust all the days of your life. And I will put enmity between you and the woman, and between your seed and her seed. He shall bruise your head. And you shall bruise His heel" (Gen. 3:14-15).

This last part is translated well in the *New International Version* as: "he will crush your head, and you will strike his heel." This emphatic statement, in any translation, is God's solemn declaration of war.

The devil had already been waging war. That's how the Fall happened. What he does in the garden is recruit not only Adam and Eve to join him in his rebellious army, but all of their children with them. Before God even enters the garden the battle lines have already been drawn. It's not as if God's approach elicits glee in the hearts of Adam and Eve, as they look for Him to punish the serpent. On one side of the battlefield stands God. On the other stands the devil, Adam, and Eve. But what is God's promise? He does not say to the serpent, "You know, my good friends Adam and Eve and I are going to get you before everything is said and done." Instead God promises that He "will put enmity between you and the woman, between your seed and her seed."

The only way Adam and Eve can change sides in this battle is if God, in His grace, should put enmity in their hearts against the serpent. After the Fall, we are friends—indeed children—of the serpent, and are by nature at enmity with God. But once the change of sides has been made, Adam and Eve will not leave the battlefield and they will fight *for* rather than *against* their Maker. With the cryptic allusion to the bruising of the heel of the seed of the woman we are given, right after the fall into sin, the first hint of the gospel. In fact, theologians refer to this promise as the *proto-gospel*, the first gospel.

But it is more than that. This passage also marks what I call the *proto-eschaton*, the first hint of the end of all things. We are told not only that the serpent will bruise the heel of the seed of the woman, but that the serpent will likewise be bruised or crushed. We are told here for the first time that in the end, Jesus wins, that His kingdom wins. When Jesus enters the scene does He still tell us to "be fruitful and multiply and exercise dominion over every living thing"? Yes and no. The command of Jesus is this: "But seek first the kingdom of God and His righteousness, and all these things shall be added unto you" (Matt. 6:33). It is the same thing. The exercising of dominion over all of the created order is the same as making manifest the reign of the kingdom of God over all things. That's what Adam was made for. And that's what Eve was made for, to help Adam in this task. Not surprisingly, that's what the Bride of Christ was made for, to cooperate with the Second Adam as He fulfills His calling. The Bible, friends, is one book, and that one book is a family portrait.

We miss this, once again, because we have drunk so deeply from the wells of the world. The world has its own peculiar goal. Everyone wants marriages that are enriched, fulfilled and exciting and hopes that their children grow up to be prosperous. In fact, the world is in a mad dash in pursuit of personal peace and affluence. Sadly, too often the evangelical church it is not much different. Of course, we want our children to become Christians. But that is just an addition to the all-consuming goal, that they would attain their own personal peace and affluence. We pray that they will be Christians just like us, who have found their way in the world. But the command of God for us and for our children is not that we would find our way *in* the world, but that we would wage war *on* the world.

Isn't this just like us, and isn't this just like God? He has given us a task, a charge, a mandate. He has designed us specifically for the serving of this purpose. Families are made for this warfare. But like Adam and Eve before us, we have our own plans. We go in search of some other job to do. We seek out some source for meaning, for significance in our lives. That's why we get so confused over the family. This is why we have come to believe that the family exists for us; that we find our own self-esteem in each other, through mutual love and admiration. Of course, self-esteem rightly understood (a rare thing indeed) is appropriate. I hope that our marriages are marked by mutual love and admiration. But this is not what they are for. This is not why the family exists. We do not exist for happiness.

We're confused because while the world offers its temptations—"Don't get married so you can enjoy your freedom and joy the rest of your life"—we in the church again reform only slightly. We don't believe that we need to die to self, but rather pretend that a good Christian marriage is the only way to get that self-interested freedom, that self-referential joy. We argue that the problem with the world isn't that they serve the self, but that they serve the self poorly. To serve the self well, that takes the church. We offer marriage seminars promising that we know the key to greater joy, to greater intimacy, to greater excitement. While it may be true that monogamy is the ultimate aphrodisiac, only a fool would marry for that reason.

Earlier in this chapter I made a little quip at the expense of John Gray. He became famous with the publication of his book, *Men Are from Mars, Women Are from Venus*. I've never read the book, and I trust I never will. But I think I understand the basic premise, and I actually think there might be something to it. I think so because I am a man, and I am from Mars. No, though I am little, I am not green. Rather, I mean that I see my life in terms of challenge, of quest, of warfare, and adventure. That's what men do. It reflects the outward call of the dominion task. Men go into the jungle and turn it into a garden. Men are by nature conquerors, which is why it makes perfect sense that Jesus calls us to this task. In Him, we are *more* than conquerors. The difference is that we do this for Him, rather than for ourselves. Dominion is all about conquest; that's what we're made for. Men live for a cause, and this is the cause—the crusade to which we have been called—to make manifest the reign of Jesus Christ.

Could there be a more glorious crusade? Would you rather conquer Europe, like Napolean? To conquer the known world like Alexander the Great? To conquer the universe like Han Solo? To win the heavyweight championship of the world, like Rocky Balboa? None of that amounts to a hill of beans. The cause I'm involved in—and the cause my family is involved in—is the absolute conquest and dominion over all things for the glory of Jesus Christ. This alone can satisfy a man.

But what about wives? John Gray is partially correct here as well. Women long for intimacy. That's the way they are made. What, though, could be more intimate, more romantic, and more dramatic than a shared vision as grand as making visible the invisible reign of Jesus Christ? My dear wife and I have, so far, six little warriors. That's a lot of diapers. Do you think that my wife and I could work our way through this mountain of diapers simply by gritting our teeth and saying, "Well, I suppose this is what God wants us to do?" No, we do this because we understand that the changing of the diaper is an integral part of the quest, part of the cause. Together my wife and I are building the kingdom of God, exercising dominion, beating back the weeds of stinky diapers, tending the garden God has put us in. This is why my dear wife vacuums the floor, for it is a part of the garden she has been called to dress and to keep. But she is doing this not as raw duty, but because she understands that she is exercising dominion over the dust, for the glory of Christ. Can you beat that for intimacy, sharing in a cause together? Can you beat that for romance? This is what covenant families are called to do. This is what we are for. There is nothing more grand, nothing more glorious, nothing more exciting, nothing more consuming, nothing more binding.

It binds us also with our children. While I am raising my children to be soldiers in this great war, I am not raising them so that one day they can be soldiers. Rather, even now we fight side by side. They do not wait until they are on their own to be about the Lord's business. They are engaged in warfare right now. Every time my children walk together with me through the grocery store, every time they remember to say, "Thank you ma'am" to the lady behind the counter that gives them a cookie, they are making manifest the reign of Christ. It is not something for later, but something we share in now. Bound together as a family, we pursue the glory of God by making known the glory of His Son.

God, as always, spoke wisely when He told us it is not good that man should be alone. And He showed forth His grace in binding us together in and as families. May He continue, in His grace, to raise up faithful families, families that recognize and are obedient to their calling. May He fill His church with families that are consumed by a single passion: to seek first the Kingdom of His dear Son.

Chapter Three:

The Covenant Husband

From time to time it is my pleasure to go to different towns and different churches and speak at various conferences. There are certain ceremonies, or liturgies that tend to go almost unnoticed at conferences, unless you go to as many as I do. Before you get up to speak, you first must listen as some poor soul goes through the difficult task of introducing you. The idea is to tell those assembled that it would be a good and prudent thing that they should listen to what is about to be said, not because the organizers went to great trouble and expense to get me there, but because I'm supposed to be a fairly reliable guy. Now when the whole thing is being set up, those who are good planners and know this part of the liturgy is coming will ask, "Do you have a bio you can send us?" I do have a bio. It's a page of tiny print that lists just about everything I've ever done that doesn't cause me great shame. The introducer's job is to pick those parts he deems most relevant for his task.

Each time this happens I go through an internal struggle. Sometimes this struggle leads to a rebuke of my introducer. Most of the time he will speak of my work on this magazine or that, or mention that I wrote a book on this theme, and edited another on some other theme. Then I come forward. I typically explain that while what the introducer said was true, what was left out is actually the center of what I am. If the goal is to introduce R.C. Sproul Jr., or even if the goal were to list my greatest accomplishments it would go something like this: "R.C. is the husband of Denise, and the father of Darby, Campbell, Shannon, Delaney, Erin Claire and Maili." That is both what I do and what I am and I need to remember that. My calling from God is as a husband and a father. My identity must be determined not by well-meaning friends and not by the world around me, but by God, my Maker.

The world has its own system for determining who I am. It has me pegged as belonging to a particular demographic group. I'm lumped in with other lumpy men, and so receive emails for weight loss pills and programs. I receive flyers in the mail for products guaranteed to stop male pattern baldness. I even receive once or twice a year a catalogue of products designed specifically for the Pittsburgh Steelers fan. And one day—in the not too distant future—the AARP will have their sights on me. While I may be tempted to understand myself in light of these groups, I'm called to do otherwise. These things are not my identity at all. I have taken on a different name. Because my identity is one with a two-thousand year old Jewish carpenter, it is likewise with all others who have the same identity. And He has called me to live out that identity as a husband and as a father. To understand this, we have to go back to the Bible once again—to the dominion mandate. God has, as with Adam, given me a helper in my dear wife. But, as it was with Adam, having that helper doesn't undo the charge. I am a son of Adam, and so I am yet called to exercise dominion over the creation.

It is usually not a difficult task to get husbands and fathers to see their calling in light of the dominion mandate. It isn't a long theoretical walk from dressing and keeping a garden to the work that we do in the world. Nor is it a stretch to understand that even if we are not farmers, we still face thorns and thistles in our work. As a magazine editor, I have to deal with printers who don't keep their promises and with angry readers who are content to have their existing convictions confirmed, not challenged. When I am able to be a part of a team that can bring together wood turned into paper, and thinking turned into teaching, then I am exercising dominion. The dominion mandate relates to my work, but not *only* to my work. There is much more to it.

In the evangelical church, at least as compared to the world around us, we are fairly traditional. As the culture moves away from the biblical ideal of the family, our vision of how to solve this problem tends to be to move back to another cultural idea that is only slightly better. We recognize that our family ought not to be modeled after the hapless *Simpsons* from television. We think it would be far better to model our families in the image of *Father Knows Best*, not realizing that the one gave rise to the other. Too often we come to the issue of the role of the father as traditionalists, as conservatives, believing that the man's job is to go out and bring home the bacon. Of course we are a little accommodating to the world around us, agreeing that after we get home from work, it would be a good thing to help out with the supper dishes from time to time. We think the man is called to make the money, or the bulk thereof, to help the wife a bit with her work, and, at least in the summertime, to cook the meat outside. If we can get that done, then we've done our job.

This is a *part* of our job. Adam did bring home the bacon, in the bread he sweated out of the ground and we ought to do the same. But this is not the center of our calling. For we who are husbands and fathers, the center of our calling is not to exercise dominion out in the jungle where we make our living, but in our homes. My job in life isn't to write books or to speak at conferences. Instead my job focuses on my wife and my children. I cannot—like Samuel, or Eli, or even David—pat myself on the back for a job well done, when I fail to do well by my wife and children. Our families are not some separate slice of our lives. Instead they are the very center of our calling in exercising dominion, and in seeking the kingdom.

I'm afraid we miss this because we're sissies. We know—despite the thorns and thistles—that coaxing a living out of the ground is comparatively easy. Every man out there is willing to say, "Okay, I'll be Robert Young in *Father Knows Best*. I can do that. But dear wife, you do the family thing. You take care of that. I'll hug and kiss the kids when I get home from work, if they're still awake, but you take care of the rest." This, however, is not our calling.

We will look at the calling of the husband, at the calling of the wife, and at the calling of the children. We will see, I pray, how profoundly interrelated these roles are, and at the important distinctions between them. But first, if we are ever going to have families that honor and obey God, we have to master this point: As husbands and fathers our central task, our central garden that we are called to dress and till, is our family. Which means when you wake up every morning, you need to ask yourself these questions: "What can I do today to manifest the kingdom of Christ? What can I do today to exercise dominion in and through my family?"

This is essentially what Paul was getting at when he addressed the men in the church at Ephesus. There he gives us a picture of what it means to be a husband. "Husbands, love your wives just as Christ also loved the church and gave Himself for her" (Eph. 5:25). This is Paul's command, given under the unerring inspiration of the Holy Spirit. I've known husbands to use this difficult call as a palliative in getting their wives to swallow Paul's command to the wife. "Dear," they say, "I know it must be a difficult calling to submit to me. But can't you see that my own calling is difficult as well, that I'm supposed to love you as Christ loved the church and gave Himself for her?" The next step is to make the claim that we actually have fulfilled this calling, at least hypothetically. We might reason with our wives this way: "Suppose that I someday would take you for a vacation to New York City. Now if I took you to New York City, perhaps I might get us a room at the Waldorf-Astoria. And if that happened, it just might happen that

I would take you to see a Broadway play. Then suppose, just for the sake of this argument, that I would take you to the Four Seasons for supper. After we finished, if I were to do all this, then we would go for a walk in Central Park. We walk hand-in-hand, and naturally, I fail to notice the sun going down. After all, I'm so struck by your beauty that I don't even know if the stars are out tonight. I can't tell if it's cloudy or bright. I only have eyes for you. Now if all this were to happen, and if, as we walked along, a mugger should emerge from behind a bush, holding a gun and demanding, 'Your money or your life.' If all this were to happen, then I know with confidence, that I would step between you and the mugger, shielding you that you might escape. I would take that bullet, and die for you, if that should ever happen. Therefore, because I would give up my life in this hypothetical situation, I love you as Christ loved the church and gave Himself for her."

Is this what Paul meant when he drew the comparison between the church and Christ and the wife and husband? To ask perhaps a more difficult, and earlier question, which part of this analogy comes first? Did God institute marriage in order to reflect the reality of the relationship of Christ and His church, or did he simply use the nearly universal experience of marriage as a handy tool to explain the relationship of Christ and the church? As is so often the case, the answer is both. Marriage was designed to be a picture of Christ and His bride precisely because they both intersect in the issue of exercising dominion. Eve was given to Adam that he might fulfill the dominion mandate. And the church is given to Jesus, the second

Adam, that He might fulfill the dominion mandate, that all things might be brought under subjection.

Just as Adam's focus, however, was on his bride, so too is the focus of Jesus upon His bride. We see that, and we avoid the silly reduction of the husband's call as taking a hypothetical bullet, if we simply continue reading what Paul has to say. "He gave himself for her that He might sanctify and cleanse her with the washing of water by the word, that He might present her to Himself a glorious church, not having spot or wrinkle or any such thing, but that she should be holy and without blemish" (Eph. 5:25-27).

We miss this because we miss the work of Christ. We think that when Jesus cried out in triumph on the cross, "It is finished" that all of His work was finished. We think Jesus is merely sitting up in heaven waiting for time to end, that He is not busy about the work His Father gave Him. He finished paying for our sins, allowing the Father to judge us as righteous. But He is still about the business of sanctifying His bride. It is this, not taking the potential bullet, that is the frightening call upon husbands. Our job is to sanctify our wives, and by extension, our own children. This is a harder job than making a living, a harder job than taking a bullet. It is a lifelong, uninterrupted job, being a tool in the sanctification of your wife and children. How can we possibly do it?

We do it, I believe, by exercising the roles for our families that Christ exercises for the church. It was John Calvin who spoke of Jesus fulfilling the *munis triplex*, the three-fold role. In answer to the question,

"What offices does Christ execute as our redeemer?," the Westminster Shorter Catechism says: "Christ as our redeemer executes the offices of a prophet, of a priest and of a king, both in His estate of humiliation and exaltation." If we would be Christ to our wives and children, this is likewise *our* calling.

What, though, is a *prophet*? Our tendency is to think of the prophet simply in terms of foretelling the future, as if the prophet is a godly form of the fortuneteller. It is certainly true that from time to time God revealed to His prophets things which were to come. This, however, is not the center of what it means to be a prophet, either in the Bible, or in our homes. The function of the prophet instead was to bring to bear the word of God on His people. One way of describing the work of a prophet is that he serves as God's lawyer, which brings us back to the covenant. God sends the prophet to bring suit against His people for violating the terms of His covenant. The prophet says, "Thus sayeth the Lord, 'You have failed to keep my covenant. I told you to do this and not to do that, but you have done what you were not to do, and not done what you were to do." God then calls the mountains, the trees and the people as His witnesses, who likewise profess that they have broken covenant.

This too is what husbands are to do. We are to wash our wives with the Word, to bring to bear the Word of God in the lives of our families. When we remind our wives not to have a complaining spirit, but to rejoice in all things, we are fulfilling our prophetic role. When we remind our children as they wrestle over who will be first in some game that the first will be last and the last will be first, we are again seeking to wash away the spots and stains, to purify, to beautify the garden that is our family. We are not just cleansing our families, but doing so with the very Word of God. We cleanse from our families those thoughts, words, and deeds that do not match up with what the Word of God commands.

This job requires some of the same sacrifice that Christ shows for us. The reality is that when our wives or our children are caught up in a particular sin—when they have a spot or a wrinkle—the last thing they want from us is to be reminded of it. They want to be left alone in their sin, because just like husbands and fathers, they are sinners. Nobody likes having their spots shown up, do they? Which means that as we fulfill our prophetic role, we should not be surprised when our wives and children get mad at us. This is not a pleasant thing for a husband and father. We like to be liked. But we are not called to be liked. We are called to be faithful. The work of the prophet is almost always lonely work, and not appreciated.

The prophet's mantel, however, is not all we are called to pick up. The second role we take as Christ to our family, as fathers and husbands, is the role of the *priest*. We need to be careful here. Here is where to some degree, the analogy breaks down. Husbands are like Christ, and wives like the church, but there is not a one-to-one correspondence. We are called to be Christ-like, but we cannot do all that Christ did. We cannot, and it would be blasphemy to even try to, atone for the sins of our family. Christ as our priest is also our substitute. He not only makes sacrifice for us, but is our sacrifice. Husbands, though they must live sacrificial lives, do not atone for their families.

But there is more to the priestly role than the making of sacrifice. A prophet is one who brings the Word of God to His people. A priest is one who brings the word of the people to God. As fathers and husbands, we must bring our families daily before the throne of God, before His mercy seat. We are, as Moses did for the children of Israel, to plead with God on behalf of our families. When I put my children to bed each night, like most Christian parents, I pray with and for my children. Every night I ask, "Lord, please bless these children." Now, what do I mean by "bless"? Am I asking God that He would let the children find the winning lottery ticket along the side of the road? Of course not. The blessing I seek for my children is that they would grow in grace, that they would show forth, in greater and greater abundance, the fruit of His Spirit. I pray that He would make my children great and mighty warriors in the great battle to which He has called all of us.

I am rather like Job who made sacrifices for his children, coming before the Lord for them. When we still had only a few children, even the posture of our praying communicated the priestly role of the father. At the conclusion of our nightly family worship I would take the children into my lap, put my arms around them, and place my hands on their heads. In so doing I am communicating to the children, "I am your covenant head. I am your God-ordained protection and shield. As your priest I will bring you before the presence of our Lord."

Husbands, this is not just for the children. I would venture to guess that there is nothing your wife wants more from you than that you should do the same for her, to pray with and for your wife. Wives crave intimacy, and nothing is more intimate than coming together before our King in prayer. This is better than buying flowers, greater than remembering to pick up your towel, more powerful than diamonds and pearls. Nothing will communicate more clearly your love for your wife than when she hears you beseech the God of heaven and earth for her. If we would be a prophet, we must also be a priest, interceding for our families, even as our Lord intercedes for us.

Being a *king*, we men figure, is a piece of cake. It's good to be the king. But we have to remember for what we have been made the king in our home. A king is the covenant head over the kingdom, which is far more about responsibility than it is about privilege. In our fourteen years of marriage, my dear wife and I have been on three different cruises. We like to cruise, at least when we're not *on* the cruise. Usually, once we board, we wonder why we're there. Cruise ships are true technological marvels. Most of the commercial cruise ships carry over two thousand guests and over one thousand staff. That's bigger than my hometown, by a factor of fourteen. They are essentially cities that float. Each ship that we traveled on had one big dining room. Each meal had two sittings, so the room itself held one thousand dining passengers.

Overseeing this floating city is the captain of the ship. He serves as the king. The reason, in fact, that ships captains are authorized to perform wedding ceremonies is connected to this idea. In the open seas there are no laws, no governments. The captain then is the sovereign on the sea, and therefore can perform weddings. But with that high privilege comes enormous responsibility.

When I sit down to eat in that dining room, if my spoon is greasy, that responsibility falls on the bus boy, on the headwaiter, on the maitre d', on the head of dining, and fully and finally on the captain of the ship. He, because he is head over everything, answers for everything. So it is for the husband and father.

Every spot and every wrinkle on your wife and children is the king's responsibility. I know this is scary, a weight we don't want. But here too, the king is called to face up to the scary things. That it is scary doesn't change that it is real. You cannot escape your responsibilities as a husband and father simply because they scare you. You can't quit. But it is also important for husbands to remember that we are also the bride. That is, as the church, we have a husband in Christ. He has promised to cleanse us, to purify us. In Him we find the strength to fulfill the very call He gives us as husbands. Unlike us, this husband has all power. Unlike us, this husband is perfectly righteous. Unlike us, this husband has infinite grace to shower on us. The answer to the fear is not to cower in our bunker, but to pray for courage. May our King stiffen our resolve, expand our vision, and equip us unto every good work.

CHAPTER FOUR:
THE COVENANT WIFE

Years ago one of my responsibilities in working with my father was to help plan out the content of his radio program, *Renewing Your Mind*. I didn't tell him what to say, mind you. I simply made suggestions of things it would be good for him to talk about. He, of course, is capable of teaching well on a variety of subjects. We recorded series on particular books of the Bible, historical series, theological series, even philosophical series. But among my favorites, and based on the response from listeners, among their favorites, was a series of broadcasts focusing on what we called "The Hard Sayings." We did a week or so of shows on "Hard Sayings of the Old Testament," another on "Hard Sayings of Jesus," and still another on "Hard Sayings of the Prophets."

A "saying" could qualify as being "hard" in one of two ways. First were those hard sayings that were difficult to understand. What could it possibly mean when Peter tells us that Jesus "preached to the spirits in prison" (1 Pet. 3:19)? But another type were those passages that were easy to understand, yet hard to swallow. When God destroys Nadab and Abihu for offering strange fire in His presence, we understand what happened, but are still shocked by it. In like manner, we are preparing to deal with a passage that is abundantly clear, but extremely difficult to swallow. It is that passage that I call the "Yes, but..." passage, because as evangelicals, we have to say "yes" to it, but we want to kill it with a thousand qualifications. The passage is Ephesians 5, verses 22 through 24: "Wives, submit to your own husbands, as to the Lord. For the husband is head of the wife, as also Christ is head of the church; and He is the Savior of the body. Therefore, just as the church is subject to Christ, so let the wives be subject to their own husbands in everything."

We cannot, no matter how much we'd like to, escape the plain meaning of Paul's injunction here. Nor can we, if we want to hold onto the authority of the Bible, dismiss this as simply being Paul's injunction. These are God's words. That's why we have to say "yes". We must concede that God calls wives to submit to their own husbands, but we are told it doesn't mean this, or it doesn't mean that, until finally we are left with wives doing whatever they want.

There is, however, at least one qualification that does not fall into the category of attempting to wiggle out from under the command of God. How are wives to submit to their husbands? "As unto the Lord." In case you're not clear on this, Paul makes it terribly clear for us. The submission that is being called for here isn't merely submission that the church actually demonstrates to Christ, but the genuine submission that the church is commanded to offer to Christ.

We have difficulty with this in large part because we live in an individualistic age. The world around us is steeped in egalitarianism. Egalitarianism is a fancy way of saying "equal-itarianism." It is a philosophy that affirms—as the Declaration of Independence does—that all men are created equal. But egalitarianism fails to include appropriate qualifiers as to the nature of that equality. It affirms not only that all people are equal before the law, not only that all people are equal in dignity and value, not only that all people are made in the image of God, but that all people are equal in authority, in relationships, and with respect to roles. This drives us to add the "buts" to Paul, but it comes from a failure to distinguish between role and ontology.

Ontology, I know, is not a word we use every day. It is part of the language of philosophers. It means of, or pertaining to, being. We get confused on submission because we, at least in this context, can't see a distinction between the role and the thing itself. Because of this confusion, we think that when God calls wives to submit to their husbands, that this is the same as God saying that women are less than men. We think submission equals less value, less dignity, less being made in the image of God. Our solution to this confusion, too often, is to deny the plain teaching of Scripture. We don't want the Bible to teach that women are less valuable or less important than men (which is a good thing because the Bible doesn't teach this). And because we think that is what is being said here in Ephesians, we look for ways to escape it. We try to undo what Paul is saying.

The better solution is to go once again back to the beginning, to how God created man. It was God Himself who said, "It is not good that man should be alone; I will make him a helper comparable to him" (Gen. 2:18). Some translations say, in an older style of English, a helper "meet" to him. "Meet" means fitting or appropriate. What you see in this language is the very point I'm belaboring. There is at the same time an equality and a distinction. Eve is made to be a helper to Adam. This affirms that she is in a position of submission. (This is made all the more clear when Adam names his wife, as naming was a sign of authority.) But at the same time, we are told that this helper is comparable to him. This speaks to the other side of the equation—her value, her dignity, her worth; in this way she is equal to Adam. Like Adam, she is made in the image of God. Thus it makes sense that God would say, "In His image He created him; male and female created He them" (Gen. 1:27).

If this isn't sufficient to put to rest the egalitarian error, there is only one place left to go. We've gone all the way back to the beginning, but now we have to go back before the beginning. We have to go back to the very first covenant. This covenant, however, is not the dominion mandate. Rather it is a covenant made among the members of the Trinity, what theologians call the *covenant of redemption*. I venture to guess that if we were to poll professing Christians about the covenant of redemption, most if not all of them would suggest that this is God's covenant with man, whereby our sins are atoned for by Christ at Calvary, and His righteousness becomes ours by faith. They would think we were talking about how we have peace with God. Technically speaking, however, the covenant of redemption isn't how we have peace with God. It is not even a covenant between God and man. Instead, the first covenant was made among the members of the Trinity.

We affirm that in His counsels before all time the Father spoke to the Son something like this: "This is the plan; this is what we're going to do. I'm going to elect a people for you, a bride. Son, you're going to take on flesh and you're going to tabernacle among them. You will obey all of my revealed will, keeping my law. But, you will receive the wrath due to the sons of disobedience. I will curse you, forsake you, such that those whom I have chosen will have their sins covered. Your righteousness will be deemed their righteousness." The Father then explained to the Spirit His role, that He would give life where there was only death, to those whom were chosen, that He would indwell those whom He had quickened, and that He would lead these same to greater and greater obedience, to reflect more and more the character of Christ.

Who is giving the orders here? In the covenant of redemption it is clearly God the Father. The Son is in a subordinate role to the Father. It seems that in John's gospel, every time you turn around there is Jesus saying: "I'm doing My Father's will," "I'm speaking My Father's words," "Whatever My Father says to do, that's what I'm going to do; whatever My Father says to say, that's what I'm going to say." In like manner, the Spirit is subordinate to the Father and the Son. Both the Father and the Son send forth the Spirit. Should we then conclude that somehow the second person of the trinity is less than the Father in terms of dignity, power, and glory, or that God the Holy Spirit is somewhat lacking, at least in comparison to the Father and the Son, in holiness, in graciousness, or in sovereignty? Of course not.

We need to understand that as the Father is making these assignments in the covenant of redemption, He is not doing so on the basis of particular strengths or weaknesses. It's not as though He is thinking: "Well, you know the Son has always been so good at being self-less. I'll incarnate Him. And don't I do wrath well? And the Spirit, He's a sweet guy. Let's have Him do the indwelling part." No, the roles are not assigned on the basis of differences among the members of the Trinity, simply because there aren't any differences. There is no attribute or perfection that you can predicate to one member of the Trinity that you cannot likewise predicate to all the members of the Trinity. In their being, they are the same.

This helps us to understand the relationship between husbands and wives. When Paul commands wives to submit to their husbands as unto the Lord, he is not saying wives are less important, that they're less valuable, that they are less able than their husbands. Wives need to understand this, lest they buck under this command. And husbands must understand this lest they lord it over their wives. God didn't say: "Well, the husbands are the smarter, stronger, wiser, more godly ones. Therefore I'll put them in charge." Rather we are talking about roles. This is about what we are called to do, not about what we are.

There is yet another important qualifier to this passage. Paul tells us that wives are to submit to their own husbands. This is not an issue having to do with the relationship between men and women, but between husbands and wives. Paul does not teach that all men have authority over all women, or that all women must submit to all men. It is quite clear that such is not the case. Wives cannot submit to other men, because they must submit to their own husbands. No one can serve two masters. This means I can't pick out any woman and say, "I want you to make me some bacon and eggs", and when she refuses I answer, "I'm a man, and you are a woman, so get busy." I am a man, but only one woman has been called to be submissive to me—my dear wife.

Then there is a third appropriate qualification. Wives are commanded to submit to their own husbands "as unto the Lord." We've already covered the four different institutions that God has created: individuals, families, states and churches. Remember also that God has established tools for exercising authority for each of these institutions. The individual is governed by the conscience; the family is ruled by the rod; the state rules through the sword; and the church rules through the power of the keys—the exercise of church discipline. Each of these exist as aids to our obedience to the one true authority, God Himself.

But there is a problem. Each of these God-ordained hierarchies involve people who are not Jesus, who are not sinless. Nevertheless, here we have the command to wives that they submit to their own husbands as unto the Lord. That is both a *description* of the submission, and a *restriction* on that submission. Remember what happened when John and Peter were commanded by those in authority to cease preaching in the name of Christ? Their response was at the same time simple, yet profound: "Judge for yourselves whether it is right in God's sight to obey you rather than God" (Acts 4:19). There is a limitation to all authority, save the authority of God Himself. None of the authorities which He has established can command us to do what He forbids, or forbid us to do what He commands.

If, for instance, I were to say to my dear wife, "What I want you to do is to walk down to the First National Bank. When you get there, blow up the door, walk in, and take all the cash you can find. I'm thinking about buying a new camper." Suppose then my wife responds, "Well, I'm not sure I can do that." I cannot then instruct her, "Look—turn in your Bible to Ephesians 5." Her duty would be to disobey me, and to obey God's injunction against stealing. This, you understand, is not an invitation to anarchy, a blank check that qualifies this command out of existence. Peter never said to the authorities, "I will have no government over me except God." We can recognize legitimate authority even when we disobey its illegitimate command to do what God forbids.

Our next qualifier is perhaps the most difficult, and is built once again around this concluding phrase, "as unto the Lord." This not only tells us that there are circumstances where wives must not obey their husband, but also tells us that when they obey, with what spirit they ought to obey. A begrudging obedience is no obedience at all. We as the church do not respond to the Lord's commands, "Well, if you say we have to do it, we suppose we have to do it." The submission of a wife to her husband ought to reflect the same joy that we are called to in our submission to our King.

But there is a third point we ought not miss about that pregnant phrase, "as unto the Lord." This, as with all that we have looked at, ties back into the dominion mandate. That is, it is important for husbands to remember for what goal we are working. The purpose behind the submission of the wife is not so that we who are husbands might enjoy the benefits of a personal servant. Paul isn't saying here, "Now you wives- this is what I want you to do: when your husband gets home I want you to have him lie on a bunch of pillows while you fan him with a palm frond and drop dried figs into his mouth." Rather, this submission is in the goal of the exercise of dominion, for the building of the kingdom. Husbands and wives are working together, the wife submissive to the husband, on the grand and glorious goal of making manifest the reign of Christ.

Just as with the members of the Trinity, while there is an equality of value, and a distinction of authority, there is also a distinction in calling. While husbands and wives work together in the building of the kingdom, their work is not identical. We see something of this in Paul's letter to Titus where he writes: "These older women, likewise, that they be reverent in behavior, not slanderers, not given to much wine, teachers of good things—that they admonish the young women to love their husbands, to love their children, to be discreet, chaste, homemakers, good, obedient to their own husbands that the word of God may not be blasphemed" (Titus 2:3-4). We considered together already the baleful propensity in the culture, and in the church, to tear families apart, to divide people into demographic groups. The above is one of the very few places in Scripture where God Himself makes demographic distinctions. He talks about older women, and He talks about younger women. What is different is that God doesn't separate them, but brings them together. God charges the older women to teach the younger women to be godly wives and mothers, to tend the garden that is the home.

This passage, as with Ephesians 5, tends to draw still more "Yes, buts..." in our day. We complain that this homeward calling is not challenging, it's not glamorous, it's not important, it's not profitable. And surely if it is none of those things, it cannot be God's calling. But this again is bucking under the authority of God Himself. He instructed Paul to instruct the older women to instruct the younger women to be homemakers. Which means that this calling comes from God Himself. Which means that not only must we obey, but that it is in fact important. If it comes from God it cannot be any more important. It cannot be any more glamorous. It cannot be any more profitable.

Only the devil could convince us to look at this call as demeaning. Both husband and wife are called to build the kingdom. Men have the principal call of going out into the jungle and turning it into a garden. Women have the principal call to tend that which is the garden. Which means this—women have the blessing of focusing their energies on raising up godly seed. Even the world sees the importance of this task, when they say: "He who rocks the cradle, rules the world." My job requires me to be hunched over a computer, or proofreading. My wife gets to spend her time laboring in God's vineyard on that which we know will last forever, our covenant children.

Of course these lines are not utterly discreet. I'm very much involved in the lives of my children, and in fact will answer for my labors in raising them in the nurture and admonition of the Lord. But the sum and substance of my wife's work is the children. What she is working on will never go out of print. What she's working on likewise talks back, and gives hugs and kisses and says, "Mommy, I love you." That's a glorious calling.

I'm afraid that because we have allowed the world to shape our thinking, we miss that glory. We in the church have bought into feminism, not principally because women rebelled against the authority of their husbands, but because husbands haven't valued the beauty of the call to be a wife and mother. Men are the ones who have treated homemaking as unimportant and insignificant. This is utter foolishness. This is self-destruction. When we buy into the modern myth that meaning for women is found outside the home, we are distracted from the business of building the kingdom. We are living in the center of the curse upon Eve—that her desire would be for her husband.

If we would be godly families, we need a spirit of rebellion, a spirit that says to the wisdom of this world, "We will not have you to rule over us." We need a thorough reformation, one that sees the beauty of the call to homemaking. May God grant us the grace to have the courage to stand against the world and, in so doing, to bring honor to our Husband, Jesus Christ.

Chapter Five:
The Covenant Child

God has not only been gracious to me by giving me such a wonderful wife, He has likewise graced both of us with six wonderful children, so far. My dear wife and I homeschool our children, and so I have given some thought to that which I want to teach them. Though not all our children are "school age", all of our children are schooled. They are all taught by my wife and me. The center of all that we teach, of course, is God's Word. I want my children to master the content of Scripture. The Bible alone is altogether true. But even this doesn't quite narrow things down enough for very small children. While we in some sense begin their education in Genesis—the book of beginnings; the first Scripture passage we hide in their hearts is found in the New Testament. No, we do not begin with John 3:16. From the time the children learn to speak, we begin teaching them this verse: "Children, obey your parents in the Lord, for this is right" (Eph. 6:1). I pray that what motivates us is not simply that we want our children to refrain from causing us trouble in their disobedience. Rather, we begin here because this is the center of God's calling in the life of children. This—obeying Mommy and

Daddy—is what God calls children to do. And just as with the issue of wives submitting to their own husbands, this passage ought to be perfectly clear.

Easy to understand and easy to obey, however, are two radically different things. Ironically, one of the reasons my children commit this passage to memory so well is because they hear it so often in the context of their *disobedience*. When one of our children disobeys, the process of discipline begins by taking the child to a private place. There I look at the child and ask, "What does God say?" That is their cue. They know they are to respond, and they always do, "Children obey your parents in the Lord for this is right." They do not puzzle over it. They have not forgotten it. Still, though, they seem often to find it easy to disobey it.

There is a reason for this disobedience to the clear, uncomplicated command of God. My children come by their disobedience naturally. You see, their daddy is not only a daddy, but a child. I have a heavenly Father. He has commanded that I should obey Him at all times and in all circumstances. But I don't obey Him. Of course, I too come by it naturally. My own earthly father has the same problem. Our children disobey us, and in doing so disobey God because they are sinners. And they are sinners because we are sinners. Sinning is easy. Obedience is tough.

But we need to not lose sight of what is easy here in this passage. There is a simplicity to the command of Paul here. There is one charge to the children, not dozens of them. Paul doesn't say that the call of children is to get straight A's at school, to be the captain of the football team, and to obey parents. Neither does Paul write to the children, "This is what I want you to do—I want you to clarify your values. It is vital that you wrestle with the great ethical conundrums of our day, and when, having done so, you emerge with the right answers, then you'll know what to do." God doesn't burden children in this way. What does God require of the child? That they obey their parents in the Lord.

This is what children were made for. Just as with the struggle wives have in submitting to their own husbands, so here the tension is between our created nature and our fallen nature. It is because we are sinners that we sin. It is because they are sinners that our children find it difficult to obey. But as children, in their "back-to-the-garden" nature, they were designed to follow. As we help them learn to obey, we are leading them back to their original nature, and away from their fallen nature.

Of course we need to remember again that, just as husbands sin, so too do parents sin. That is, the authority of parents has a limit here. How are children to obey their parents? "In the Lord." The principle is the same as with the wife. It is the duty of children to obey their parents unless or until the parent forbids the child to do what God commands, or commands the child to do what God forbids. If I were to say to my son, "Campbell, I want you to go down and rob the bank, because I need a new truck to pull my new camper," he must not respond, "Well, I'm a child, and therefore I am not responsible. My duty to obey God leads me only to my duty to obey my father. I will go rob the bank." While surely in such a scenario my guilt would outweigh my son's guilt, nevertheless, his duty would be to disobey my orders, in obedience to God.

The difficulty with this section of Ephesians 6 is not in the instruction Paul gives to the children. Rather, the hard part is when Paul turns his attention back to the parents, especially to the fathers. Paul continues: "Honor your father and your mother, which is the first commandment with promise, that it may be well with you, and you may live long on the earth" (Eph. 6:2-3). By the way, the second verse my children learn is Exodus 20:12, which Paul quotes here. They get a double whammy of God's call to children to honor and obey their parents. "And you, fathers, do not provoke your children to wrath, but bring them up in the training and admonition of the Lord" (Eph. 6:4).

Isn't it interesting how swiftly Paul moves from addressing the children to addressing the father? I believe this is still more evidence of what we looked at earlier. The father is indeed the king in his home. Which means he is responsible for all that goes on in the home. He will answer for his labors in teaching the children to obey their parents. It is a burden on the father, but one that we cannot escape.

That doesn't mean, however, that we don't try to escape. Fathers here have their own version of the "Yes, but..." problem. But this "but" is right there in the text. Fathers are not to provoke our children to wrath, but to bring them up in the training and admonition of the Lord. What we often do with this is turn it upside down. We think that Paul is essentially saying: "Fathers, you need to make sure that your children obey. But be careful not to overdo it. You know what happens when you are too strict with the children, don't you? It causes them to rebel. What you need to do is leave some room in which your children can go out and sin, and disobey. Give them free reign when they turn two. Expect them to be rebellious in their teens. Don't clamp down, or it will only make it worse."

This understanding of this passage is not only bad exegesis, it is bad grammar. We do not want to provoke our children to wrath. How do we make sure we don't do that? By raising them in the training and admonition of the Lord. The opposite of not provoking your children to wrath is not making sure that they obey. Instead, we provoke our children to wrath when we do not make sure that they obey. What brings the wrath is not our thoroughness in raising the children in the training and admonition of the Lord, but our sloppiness. Our job as fathers is crystal-clear—to raise the children in the training and admonition of the Lord. We are not called to find some happy medium between obedience and disobedience. We're not called to command some obedience, but not too much. How do you provoke your children to wrath? You do it first by failing to discipline them. We will consider some principles of sound discipline in another chapter.

It is important to remember that Paul's admonition is rather specific. The last part of verse 4, "the training and admonition of the Lord" is sometimes translated nurture and admonition, sometimes fear and admonition. The Greek word which is translated "training," or "nurture," or "fear" is *paideia*. The root of this word is grounded in the idea of culture. What Paul is enjoining here is that we would bring our children up in the *culture* of the Lord. Throughout this book we have seen how the serpent seeks to get us to think his thoughts after him. He wants your children to look at God, at themselves, at their families, at the world around them in a certain way. But God, in making covenant with families, tells us that our job as parents is to raise them in His world, in His culture, in His kingdom, on His side in the great battle between the seed of the woman and the seed of the serpent. That's what the *shema*, the most sacred text of the whole Bible to the Old Testament Jews, is all about. "Hear, O Israel. The Lord your God, the Lord is one. You shall love the Lord your God with all your heart, with all your soul and with all your strength" (Deut. 6:4-5). What comes next? "And these words which I command you today shall be in your heart. You shall teach them diligently to your children, and shall talk of them when you sit in your house, when you walk by the way, when you lie down and when you rise up" (vss. 6-7). God is telling His people to teach the children, teach the children, teach the children. Tell them who God is, what God has done, and what God requires of us. That's what it means to raise them in God's culture, and what a glorious culture it is. Our lives—both ours and our childrens—are all about the glory of the kingdom of God.

Our family tradition begins at birth. When God blesses us with a daughter—which He has now done five times—after she is cleaned up, after Mommy gets to hold her, after they wrap her up tight like a loaf of bread, the nurses always put the baby in the bun warmer, the tiny little bassinette on wheels with a heat lamp. That's when it's my turn. I take my Bible, and go to my daughter and speak these first words to her: "Darby" (or Shannon, or Delaney, or Erin Claire or Maili), "This is Daddy, and I want to read something to you." I open my Bible to Proverbs 31, to that beautiful portrait of a godly woman, and read it. "This," I then explain to my minutes-old little girl, "is your calling. This is what Mommy and Daddy will be training you to be." My son received essentially the same talk, except that I read to him from Proverbs 3.

The training continues as we teach our children their first song. You are probably familiar with it. It goes, "Father Abraham had many sons. Many sons had Father Abraham. I am one of them, and so are you. So let's just praise the Lord." What am I teaching my children? I'm giving them their identity. I'm telling them of their culture, that we are the children of Abraham, that the Bible is not just our rule book, but it is also our family history. I am telling my children that it was their great-great-great-great, I don't know how many greats, grandfather, Noah, whom God spoke to and told to build an ark.

I'm giving my children an identity separate from the one established for them by pop culture. I'm giving them the identity that we share together as one family, because we are together in covenant with God. We do much the same thing in what we like to call our family liturgy. It goes something like this. I will ask those of my children who can speak, "What is your name?" They give me their first name. "What is your other name?" They then give me their second name. "What is your last name?" They answer, "Sproul." Then I ask them this, "What are Sprouls?" And they reply, "Sprouls are free." Do my children have a profound understanding of freedom? Of course not. They are little children. But they will grow into that knowledge because they have been taught that this is their identity.

I ask them next, "Whom do Sprouls fear?" And they reply with gusto, "Sprouls fear no man—Sprouls fear God." This is our ontology, our being. This is what we are, all of us. Finally, I ask them, "Whom do Sprouls serve?" They respond, "Sprouls serve King Jesus."

I am called to raise my children in the culture of the Lord. That means I must teach my children who they are. I must explain to them their identity, and that their identity is the same as my identity, and their mother's identity. In so doing, I am instructing them on how to live within God's culture. I'm giving them a vision for building God's kingdom.

As is always the case, however, we are not called to obey with grim determination and a stiff upper lip. Obedience to God, in all circumstances, is an invitation to joy. This is why we teach our children to obey, that it might go well for them in the land where God has put them. This is the promise inherent in the fifth commandment, in Exodus 20:12. Honoring our father and our mother is not just a good way to avoid the wrath of God, but is a great way to enjoy His blessing.

That promise does not stop once the children have grown. When I am teaching my smaller children to memorize Exodus 20:12, "Honor your father and your mother that you may have a good life" ("that you may have a good life" is from a small children's paraphrase version), I give them just a smidgen of commentary. Our liturgy here goes like this: I ask them, "What does God say?" "Honor your father and your mother that you may have a good life" they happily respond. Then I ask, "What does honor mean?" They reply, "Honor means to obey." I must confess that I am taking a little liberty there. Mitigating my confession is that Paul seems to be doing much the same thing in Ephesians 6. For small children the call to honor certainly carries with it the call to obey. But what about adult children? What about children who have established their own homes? Do they have a duty to honor their parents, to obey them? Yes and no. No matter how old we get, we never lose our obligation to honor our parents. When we have established our own homes, however, we no longer are called to obey.

Consider what is happening, for instance, in most wedding ceremonies. Early on the bride-to-be is escorted down the aisle by her father. The officiating minister asks, "Who gives this bride?" The father typically answers, "I do, together with her mother" or "Her mother and I do" or some such variation. What is happening here? The young lady is moving from being under the care and authority of her parents, to being under the care and authority of her husband.

In like manner, the Scriptures tell us that a man is to leave and then to cleave. He steps out of the binding authority of his parents, and so establishes his own home. When a man and a wife come together, they create a new family. Neither the husband, nor the wife have any obligation to obey their parents. But they still must honor them. How do we do that?

Though these things are not at all clearly spelled out in Scripture, there does seem to be a pattern of leadership that stays with what we might call the patriarch of the clan. As we discussed in the first chapter, in my "clan" my parents fulfill that role. While they do not command obedience, my mother and father are the greatest counselors my wife and I have. The same is true for my sister and her husband. While I do not ask my parents' permission to do this or that, I do have a strong policy not to make any significant life decisions without consulting them. Are we thinking of moving? My dear wife, Denise, and I will talk it over with my parents. (We would, in fact, talk it over with both sets of parents.) Are we dealing with a thorny relational issue among our children? Where better to get counsel than from those who have gone before?

Please understand, however, that the blessing of receiving wisdom from our parents isn't only about what we get out of the deal. Parents, naturally, are eager to be an important part of the lives of their children, even when they are grown. They delight to dispense wisdom to their loved ones. Because they love us, they want things to go well for us. When we seek their counsel, we are affirming to them that we know that they love us and wish us well.

Another way that we honor our parents is by giving them what we have, but they lack. I don't have a great deal of wisdom to give to my parents. But I am, at least relative to them, a young man. When there is what my father calls "donkey work" to be done—lugging his suitcase out to the car, for instance—we should not only do this, but do it with joy.

The same applies with respect to the time we spend with each other. It is not an easy thing for me to load up my large family and drive through several states to see my parents and my in-laws. But it may be easier for me to do this than it is for them, as they grow older, to come here. Seeing our parents, because the honor we seek to show them comes from our hearts and not merely our wills, is something we delight to do.

We honor our parents when we do things their way, even when their way seems odd to us. My father is the man you get frustrated driving behind. He is polite, but slow and methodical. I, on the other hand, have been accused of being the man they warn you about when they tell you how important it is to drive defensively. But when I am driving my father, I try diligently to drive his way rather than my way.

This same principle ought to be taken into consideration during the worship wars that plague so many churches. If we have to chose between music that we think will make younger visitors more at ease, or music that will make our parents more at ease, is it really a choice? Should we not consider singing the songs of our fathers and grandfathers at least, if for no other reason, because they are the songs of our fathers and grandfathers?

Finally, we should be quick to speak honorably to our parents. We should tell them that it is our desire to honor them. We should have the courage to say to them, "I repent for my failures to honor you in the past. By God's grace, I purpose to honor you as God commands."

Our culture and our calling is not restrained to just one or two generations. When we honor our parents one of the best things that will go well for us is this: we are teaching our children what it means to honor us. There is wisdom in the old adage that more is caught than taught. If we lecture our children on the importance of honoring our parents, while speaking ill of our own parents, they will zero in on our inconsistency and follow the latter example, rather than the former teaching. Likewise, a good example will redound to a blessing, even to our grandchildren. As we honor our parents, we teach our children to honor us, and teach their children to honor them.

I constantly remind my children that it is not enough for them to keep some of the stipulations of the covenant. It isn't enough for them to obey part of God's law. They, in turn, must also keep this part of the covenant—they must teach these same truths to their own children. To live in the culture of the Lord is to raise children in that culture, and to raise them to do the same with their children. Our identity then transcends this generation. We are the heirs of our parents, who were the heirs of their parents, who were the heirs of their parents. And in the second Adam, we are heirs of all things. Our common calling then is to make manifest the reign of Christ, until He comes again in great glory. May God equip us to raise up godly seed in our families. May He equip our children to do the same.

May He, in fact, do mighty deeds through our children, and our children's children, for the sake of His Son and His kingdom.

CHAPTER SIX:
THE CHURCH FAMILY

As we have considered together the nature and calling of the covenant family, I wouldn't be surprised if some of you have felt a bit left out. I know that when I speak on these themes at conferences there are always people wanting to know, understandably so, "How does this apply to me?" We've seen already that the world, and the serpent are at war with the family. We have focused our attention on how the devil distorts our thinking about the family. But he has not only distorted our understanding of the family, but he has inflicted real, lasting damage to particular families. He has succeeded in tearing families apart that are meant to be bound together. Sin, we know, brought death into the world, and death has torn families apart. But it is also sin that has brought divorce into the world, and divorce tears families apart. The solution to sin—the Gospel—ironically also has the capacity to tear families apart, as Jesus Himself warned.

We have suggested in an earlier chapter that one of the great weaknesses in our day is that our understanding of the family has essentially been reduced down to the nuclear family. As bad as this is, it is far worse that there are in our day so few families still intact at the nuclear level. There are cities in America where illegitimate births outnumber legitimate births. We have more broken families now than we ever have in our history. This creates circumstances where it seems that people are alone, that they are no longer connected to a family. We have seen already that the Bible has much to say to those who are bound together in families. But does the Bible speak to those who are without families? Does it address those who are family-less?

As is so often the case, the answer is yes and no. The Bible does speak to those who, because of sin, because of death, because of divorce, because even of the Gospel, are left without biological kin. It has some very specific things to say of those who are in this kind of circumstance. But the answer is also no, because those who are a part of the church, who are the children of God, the bride of Christ, cannot rightly be understood to be family-less. If you are a citizen of the kingdom of God, then you are part of a family. All Christians are, in fact, a part of the family of God, which is the church.

We have considered together, several times, the four institutions that God has established among men: the individual, the family, the church, and the state. We have looked at how in our day the devil is seeking to expand the scope of the individual and the state and to squeeze out the mediating institutions, the family and the church. The family and the church fight a war on two fronts, as the world tries to squeeze each of them out of existence.

That ought to mean, of course, that these two mediating institutions would band together, to take common cause against their common enemies. Sadly, too often what we see instead is that these two institutions squabble over what remains of the pie. While there is a vital relationship between the family and the church, we have melded the two together where we shouldn't have, and divided them where we should have kept them together. As we consider these issues—where the church has intruded upon the family, and to a lesser extent, where the family has intruded upon the church—we should reach some wisdom on how the church is called to relate to those who are without families.

Where are we muddled on these issues? One place we get confused on the appropriate roles for the family and the church is in the church itself, where we follow the world's method of dividing up families. Just as the world has separate programs for fathers, mothers, teenagers, children, and toddlers, we have the same in the church. When we separate husbands from wives, when we pull apart parents from their children, we essentially divide up the church. We no longer have one church, but have a tiny children's church, a men's church, and a ladies' church. We hire professionals at the church, and thereby encourage men to abdicate their responsibilities for the spiritual growth and well-being of their families.

It also happens, however, the other way. There are families out there, many of which have become frustrated with the attempts by local churches to divide up their families, who make the opposite error of thinking they can be the church, by themselves. There is a misguided but growing movement in our day of families thinking they can be churches unto themselves. This is dangerous on many fronts.

Instead, the calling is this: The church ought to be, as the family of God, seeking the kingdom of God, trying to make manifest or visible the reign of Jesus Christ, by being a family above the family, and by being a family to the family-less.

What does it mean to be a family above the family? We've looked several times at the limitations on the authority God has given to those in positions of leadership. Remember that a child is to obey his or her parents "in the Lord." There is a line there that must not be crossed. We must, if we are forced to choose, obey God rather than men. In like manner, when Paul in Ephesians 5 commands that wives must submit to their husbands, it is "as unto the Lord." The same principle applies. No wife is to obey her husband when he insists that she violate the law of God.

This principle is founded upon the hard truth that wherever God established human authority, that human authority is beset by sin. Husbands have asked their wives to disobey God. Parents have done the same to their children. Under heaven, if there is to be authority, it will be an authority tainted by sin. But there is more to the solution than simple disobedience. Often our disputes arise when both parties insist that the law of God is on their side. Sometimes husbands fail to lead as Jesus leads.

Sometimes wives fail to follow as the church is called to follow Christ. So what do we do?

Here is where the church is to be a family above the family. God has established the church in part as a sort of court of appeals. In so doing, He has reminded us that all of us are under authority. The husband is indeed king in his home, who not only reports to Jesus in a very real, spiritual way, but also reports to Jesus in a real, spiritual way through the earthly authority that Jesus established, which is the church.

How does this work in real life? Suppose that I suddenly developed an overpowering fancy for fishing. God does tell us to exercise dominion over the fish of the sea. Imagine that I enjoy fishing so much that I come to my dear wife with this idea: "You know, dear, how much I love fishing. And you know, I presume, though you do not know it in full, that I am an outstanding fisherman. You know also that there is often tension in our home about my fishing. I want to fish, while you think it more important that I cut the grass, clean the gutters, paint the house, or fix the fence. Here's my idea. I think we need to sell the house. We can take the proceeds from the sale and buy a really fine fishing boat, lots of fishing gear, and we'll move down to the lake, and I'll just fish all the time." And Denise asks, "What do you suppose we'll live in, after we sell the house?" "Oh," I'd reply, "I have that all figured out. That's part of the beauty of the plan. We could live in a tent. Why, with the equity in our house, after the boat and the supplies, we could still afford just about the best tent there is. But it gets even better. Without the house and the yard, you won't always be asking me to do all those chores. I'll have more time to fish. Every morning I'll get up, fire up the boat, and fish all day long. What do you think?"

If I were to float this idea by my wife, she would probably respond, "Well dear, this is not, believe it or not, the worst idea you've ever had. But it's certainly in the top three." Now suppose I conclude the discussion with, "Well, dear, you know Ephesians says you are to submit to me, so I'd like you to start packing, please. Call the realtor, call the banker, and I'll start looking through the classifieds for my boat." What does she do?

Our inclination, because the command is so preposterous, is to assume some sort of vague rule of thumb. We assume that Paul must mean, "Wives submit to your own husbands unless they're out of their tree." But Paul makes no such exception. If we only submit when we agree with the wisdom of those who are in authority over us, then we never really submit at all. We're just doing what we want. So how do we help my dear wife escape? It's rather simple. All she needs to do is, and this is assuming that I refuse to hear any wisdom from her, is call our session, those who sit in the seat of authority in our local church. She calls them and asks for their help.

My wife does not have the authority to stop me from pursuing this fishing dream. But the elders of the church do have that authority. They would call me in and say, "Now, R.C., the Scripture is terribly clear that if you don't provide for your family then you are worse than an infidel. What you are proposing to do is serious sin. The Word of God says that you must be a wise steward of what God has provided for you, and you would be a foolish steward indeed if you went through with your plans. We're here to tell you not only why we think you shouldn't do it, but to forbid you to do it. If necessary we will exercise the power of the keys. If you do not repent and turn from this wicked plan, we will excommunicate you from the church of Christ."

This is what a court of appeals is supposed to do. My wife and I have a dispute. We are not agreeing. I am asking her to do something she doesn't think we ought to be doing. So she goes to court. The court she comes to however, is the church, not the state. That I am not Jesus is painfully apparent. But here, in a church that is willing to exercise discipline and recognizes its rightful calling in these circumstances, she has protection. If we were in a "church" that lacked this mark of the true church—namely, discipline—my poor wife would be on her own.

But there is a limit going in the other direction as well. Those who exercise authority in the church need to be careful. Suppose instead of planning to buy a tent and fish the rest of my life, I come home to my dear wife one day and say, "You know, I was down in Florida and I saw the neatest thing. There were several homes there that had—you won't believe this—it was just so beautiful and stunning. Right there, in their front yards where you could see it when you drove by, they had these really huge, plastic, big pink flamingoes. They were so cool. On my way back to Virginia I stopped and picked up a dozen for our yard. Boy will our neighbors be jealous."

Now what happens when my wife, who's already embarrassed by the way her husband dresses, goes to the session in the hopes of avoiding further embarrassment? I suppose my session would laugh in understanding of the trials my wife goes through because of my lack of taste, but then they might say, "You know, Denise, as much as we sympathize with you, this is not the appropriate jurisdiction for this issue. This is just not that significant of an issue to warrant our stepping in. We're sorry that you're going to have to live with a tacky yard. You've gotten used to his ties not matching his shirt. You can get used to this as well. You're going to have to get over this."

Like any court, the court of appeals that is the local session at the church, cannot afford to be bogged down with frivolous "lawsuits" among family members. In fact, when they do get involved in these petty issues, what will happen is they will micromanage the home, and leave precious little room for the husband to exercise his God-given authority. Families need to be able to work these things out. Sometime submission may mean having to put up with petty quirks and weaknesses.

Do not let all this court language, however, confuse you. Remember as we looked earlier at the nature of covenants that we argued that covenants are in some ways like contracts, but in other ways they are more akin to relationships. In fact, this is the beauty of the covenant—it marries together the legal and the familial. When we reduce things down to contracts, we've lost something. If I were intent on fishing for the rest of my life, the session doesn't send me a cold and professional subpoena telling me, "You will appear before this court on such and such a date." Instead they say to me, "Brother R.C., our friend, for whom we care, to whom we have covenanted, let's talk about this plan of yours. Please, hear the wisdom of the elders."

Of course, on the other hand, we cannot err on the side of too much family and not enough contract. If I refuse to hear the wisdom, it isn't enough for the older gentlemen in the church to simply say, "We think your plan isn't such a good one" and leave it at that. We ought not to split asunder what the covenant has brought together. We need both the enforcing of the law and the tender care of the family.

The church is not only called to be a family above the family, it is also called to be a family to those who have no family. The Scripture speaks of these folks, and we would do well to recover the language of the Bible. The Bible calls those without family "widows and orphans." If we simply remembered that, we would not only see that the Bible does in fact address the family-less, but that we are called to show forth to them an extra measure of grace.

Paul wrote to Timothy, "Honor widows who are really widows. But if any widow has children or grandchildren, let them first learn to show piety at home and to repay their parents; for this is good and acceptable before God" (1 Tim. 5:3-4). What is Paul saying? Is he guilty of redundancy, or of doubletalk when he writes of widows who are really widows? How can one be a widow without being a widow? In this context, one could be a widow without being a widow. What Paul is doing is distinguishing between two different kinds of widows. On the one hand are those who yet have other family. They have no husbands, but they do have families. This is the first line of defense. Of course, here is one place the state has crept in where it does not belong. Widows in our day are instructed to turn to the state for their care. Not so according to the Bible. First it is the extended family.

The second group of widows, widows indeed, are those who have no extended family. This is a woman with no husband, and no family. And Paul's instructions are rather clear here: The church must become a family to the widow. If possible, the solution is to help the widow become a non-widow, that she might remarry. I am puzzled over why we don't see this happening very often in the church.

If remarriage, however, is out of the question, this is where the church steps in. The church becomes the family to the family-less. We are to care for these women, tend to them, take care of their needs. The Bible, however, not only tells us what we are to do here, but tells us also how important it is that we do this. James tells us, "Pure and undefiled religion before God and the Father is this: to visit orphans and widows in their trouble and to keep oneself unspotted from the world" (James 1:27). I'm afraid we fail to visit orphans and widows in their trouble precisely because we *are* spotted by the world. James is telling us here that this is not a peripheral matter. We cannot slough off these duties and still claim to be within the one true faith. This is not an option; yet I'm afraid we as the church rarely fulfill this mandate.

I understand how difficult this can be. The church that I serve, Saint Peter Presbyterian Church, is a rather small church. When we were confronted with this situation, we were a tiny little church. We had a young married couple in our church with two small children. After about four years of marriage, the husband decided he had had enough, and so packed his bags and left. The session of the church called upon the man to repent of his sin. He refused, and so in due time, he was excommunicated from the church. He was told that as far as we were concerned, he was dead to us, unless or until he repented. At this time our church didn't even have ten families, and now one of them was without a husband and father. Not only that, but the infidel father, from the time he left, even to this day as far as I know, did not send a single dime to support his wife and children.

What could we do? Our session met and reasoned together, "We're a tiny, struggling church. We're barely past being a mission church. We have hardly any families, hardly any money. But God tells us precisely what we are supposed to do. We will care for this woman and her dear children. That's what we must do." We ended up buying a trailer. We put the woman and her children in that trailer and told her, "You send us the bills. We will pay for your groceries, your lot rent, your phone, electricity, water—whatever you need, we as a church will pay for it. That's what we're called to do."

It happened, in the providence of God, that the trailer we bought was right next to one owned by another family in the church. The wife of that family was quite friendly with our widow, and the husband a fine, godly young man. The session gave him a job to do. When the widow needed a drain unclogged, it was his duty to get it done. In the evenings, when he gathered his own small family together for family worship, he was to include the widow and her children. When the children were unresponsive to the discipline of the mother, he was to exercise discipline there as well. He was to be a father and a husband to this family in very ordinary, practical, and natural ways. Because of his character, he was able and willing to perform these duties. And in so doing he modeled for the little boy what a godly man acted like.

Word got out about what we were doing for this family. It did not surprise us that the world was stunned by our decision. We didn't expect them to understand our convictions. What surprised our church, however, was how we surprised the other churches in the area. One would have thought that we in our church were little green men from Mars. We were asked, "What is this? What are you doing? Are you insane?" That ended up being perhaps the hardest part of what we went through, accepting the incredulity of too many churches around us. Of course we were encouraged as well, as many churches also helped us to carry the load financially.

It was a hard thing for the widow. We weren't, of course, able to keep her in great style. She had to trust that the church would meet her needs. The state offered to do the same. She had to choose one or the other, because we as a church had no interest in helping the state care for her. It was tough on her pride. But I reminded her that her calling at that time was to be Jesus to us, that we might have the opportunity to be Jesus to her. We cannot give a cup of water in the name of Christ, unless there are those in our midst who have need of a cup of water. He called her to be thirsty, that He might call us to give her drink.

One need not wait, of course, for needs to get quite this dramatic. I venture to guess that each of us, somewhere in our home church, have those who, if not being widows indeed, are at least not overflowing to abundance in terms of family. There are single women who might need to have a flat tire changed. There are older women who might need to have their lawn mowed from time to time. There is no reason churches cannot go and become fathers to the fatherless, husbands to the husbandless. In fact, there is every reason for us to do so. It's not terribly complicated. The widows will be pleased. The orphans will be pleased, and the world will be shocked. Not least God commands it, and God likewise will reward our obedience.

I told our widow that as hard as it was on her, it was a delight for us as a church to meet her needs, and the needs of her precious children. It was a delight because of our genuine love for her, and for them. We had vowed when she joined the church to love her. We had vowed when her children were baptized to aid her in raising them in the nurture and admonition of the Lord. We had no choice. But as is so often the case, obedience was for us a joy. No experience in the short life thus far of our church has more tightly bound us together as the body of Christ.

My prayer is that such will happen all across the spectrum within the church of Christ. Let us by all means recover what James calls "pure and undefiled religion." This is not a substitute for the Gospel of Jesus Christ, but its necessary outworking. May the Spirit that gives us life, give us the grace to be families to those who are without families, that our heavenly Father would be pleased.

Chapter Seven:
Withhold Not
Correction

God warns fathers that we must not provoke our children to wrath (Eph. 6:4). One simple way of translating this concept is to believe that God warns fathers against making their children mad. Such an understanding would be mad indeed. God warns instead that we, as we seek to help our children learn to obey, that we do not instead lead them toward destruction. The text isn't telling us that if we overdo the discipline that our children will be provoked to wrath. Nor is it promising us that if we discipline our children that they will not be provoked to wrath. While it is not a complicated thing, we can surely discipline our children in a foolish and counter-productive way. We will surely provoke our children to wrath if we don't discipline them. But we might so provoke them even if we do. Our calling is to love our children enough to discipline them, and to discipline them with wisdom.

A critical part of that wisdom is being sure that both we and our children understand the *why* of the discipline. The question here isn't, "What did you do?" but is rather, "Why are we doing this?" Before our children can grasp the "why" we must grasp it first, which is easier said than done. I suspect I am like most parents in discerning that discipline is more apt to come out at some times than others. Suppose I am enjoying a slow Saturday morning with the children. It is my habit on these days to cook up eggs and sausages and biscuits. Now if my little girl Maili were to spill her milk, chances are that here I would gently correct her, encourage her to be more careful, and clean up the milk. Now suppose instead that it is Saturday afternoon. My favorite football team is set to kick-off in the next two minutes. I have just built an entirely too-tall sandwich. I gingerly clutch a bag of chips as I prepare to head upstairs to enjoy the game. Now Maili spills her milk. Chances are I won't have the same level of patience. Chances are my tone won't be gentle. Chances are, though there is no sense in it, that we will have both crying and spilled milk.

These different reactions demonstrate that my own goal in disciplining the children isn't correcting them for their sake, but punishing them for having the gall to inconvenience me. We face much the same kind of temptation when we consider our response to a certain behavior when we are home alone with the family, and how we respond to the same behavior when we are with friends or extended family. When we discipline our children because they have inconvenienced or embarrassed us, we are teaching them that the world runs on power, that we ought to obey those who are bigger and stronger than us. Such, of course, not only teaches them not to obey when there is no one bigger and stronger around, but teaches them to use their own power for their own purposes as they grow older.

After a spanking I will often ask my children, "Why did daddy spank you?" Their response is always the same, "To help me learn to obey." Then I ask them this question, "Why does Daddy want you to obey?" Having learned the promise of God in the fifth commandment, "Honor your father and mother that it may go well with you in the land," they reply, "That it might go well with me." I need to make sure that I and my children understand that what motivates the discipline is the heartfelt desire to see them blessed from the hand of God. Indeed, even before the spanking, the sadness I go through when my children have disobeyed is grounded in the same truth. I'm sad because my heart's desire is that their lives would go well.

It is not unduly selfish, on the other hand, for me to desire as well, that it would go well for me. But what will cause it to go well for me is not that my daughter will not spill her milk just before the big game, but that I would honor my Father in heaven. That is why I often remind the child of another passage, "Foolishness is bound up in the heart of a child; the rod of correction will drive it far from them" (Prov. 22:15). I want to remind the children and me, that I too am a man under authority. I spank them because I am not to disobey my heavenly Father. This event isn't my doing. It isn't driven by my wisdom. I too, must submit to those in authority over me. Once again, I am teaching my children that this isn't merely about power. We are an entire household of people who are required to submit. (You might want to keep this in mind as well if you are tempted to scoff at any portion of the law. When we do not buckle our seatbelts we are not merely foolishly endangering our lives. We are also teaching our children that we are not under authority, unless the authorities are watching.)

We live in a world that tells us that the rod is bad. To be sure some tragically provoke their children to wrath by crossing the line that separates discipline from abuse. But that doesn't change the plain teaching of the Word. We have experts writing learned papers for prestigious journals telling us that when we spank our children that we train them to be violent; that they will learn from the experience that problems are solved through violence. We are told that spanking damages our children. Sadly, we often tend to accommodate the wisdom of the world. We believe, because we have been taught to believe, that it takes an expert to really understand anything, rather than He who created the children in the first place. We think maybe instead of giving us the rod as a tool of enforcement, God gave us the time-out chair. It's still unpleasant after all. (I wonder why no one makes the argument that when we use the time-out chair we teach our children that time-out is the way to solve our problems.) And in so doing we make manifest our own disobedience. We likewise make manifest our own hatred for our children (Prov. 13:24). I do not need to make a case for using the rod. Here too, the Bible is abundantly clear.

If we were wise, we should also consider why we don't spank. That is, not why do we fail to spank, but what are some of the reasons that don't motivate us? This is not a side issue, but the very substance of our child-rearing. We will provoke our children to wrath unless we understand that we do not punish our children retributively. To put it more plainly, we do not punish our children for the sake of bringing justice to pass. That's not our goal. We are not, when we discipline our children, seeking to even the cosmic scales of justice. There are not only different spheres of authority, complete with different tools of enforcement, but there are also different goals, different purposes for punishment. The call of the state is to use the sword as a tool of justice. It is not appropriate for the state to see itself as a ministry of mercy. Nor is it fitting to see itself as fulfilling a teaching role. (This is one reason why the perennial debates over the restraining power of the death penalty miss the point. God did not establish the death penalty to reduce crime. He did it to see that justice is met.)

It is not justice I seek in disciplining my children. Why not? Because, if my children are His children, then justice has already been done, in mercy. If my children are His children, than the retributive justice due to my children for their disobedience was put upon Christ in His passion. Retribution was made at Calvary. Jesus has already paid the penalty for their sin. His cry, "It is finished," reaches through time to cover the sins of my believing children.

As we remember this important truth with respect to punishment, it helps us avoid the other punishments that often escape our notice. When we discipline our children, we sometimes add to the pain of the rod sundry other forms of pain. We might add a level of embarrassment.

(This is one reason that our children are not told to drop their drawers when being spanked. We are not trying to humiliate them.) Or we may use our tongues as a tool of punishment. How often do we speak unkindly to our children, hurting them with our words. Still worse is when we fail to reconcile after discipline. When we hold a grudge against our children, we punish them with a certain coldness or aloofness. This can leave scars that will last far longer than we would like.

The function of punishment is to train my children in obedience. It is rehabilitative rather than punitive. I explain to my children that I am not spanking them in order to make things right, to even out the scales of justice. Rather, I am spanking them because I want to make *them* right. That's my motivation in spanking my children, and that's also why it ought to be for us such a joyous occasion. That is why I do not need to be stern and angry during this process. It's a lesson to be learned.

I tend to look rather silly when I'm about the business of disciplining my children. I get a big goofy grin on my face, looking to all the world like some kind of twisted sadist. My biggest frustration is not when my children commit rank rebellion, but when they walk that line between obedience and rebellion. It's a trait children learn at an early age, and one, not surprisingly, that we never outgrow. We all like to dance around that line. As I man, I struggle with that temptation. As a father dealing with my own children, I hate trying to figure it out, wrestling over what I'm supposed to do. But when the disobedience is blatant and clear, then, of course, my calling is likewise clear. And it provides a powerful opportunity to train my children.

This is how discipline progresses in our home when I am doing it right. Suppose, for the sake of argument, that my son, Campbell, has shoved his sister, Delaney. How would I know this? Delaney would come to me and say, "Daddy, Campbell shoved me." I pray she comes to me because she knows I need to know these things. I pray her desire would be to see her brother grow in grace, not to see him get in trouble. I fear she may be struggling with delighting in the misery of another. My response is calm and measured, "Please go and tell Campbell to come see me in his room." Delaney at this point has a pretty good idea of what is about to happen. But she also knows that she has been summoned herself before. She faces temptation to ask me, "Is he going to get a spanking?" If she succumbs to that temptation, she will hear the same thing her brother hears should he ask if she is going to get spanked, "It's not your concern." This too, is part of trying to make sure that embarrassment isn't added to the punishment I'm soon to dole out.

Campbell enters the room, and I ask, "Campbell, did you shove your sister?"

"Yes, Daddy."

"Has Daddy told you that boys are to protect girls?"

"Yes, Daddy."

"Is shoving your sister protecting girls?"

"No, Daddy."

"What does God say, son?"

"Children obey your parents in the Lord, for this is right."

"That's right son, and you disobeyed Daddy. Daddy, who must obey God, must spank you. Why is Daddy going to spank you?"

"To help me learn to obey."

At this point I bend Campbell over my knee, and give him a thorough "SWACK!" with the spanking stick. With all appropriate caution against doing actual damage to our children, we must concede one more point here. We provoke our children to wrath if we use the rod to simply fan the fannies of our children. That it is to say, if it doesn't hurt, not only are we doing it wrong, but we are wronging the children.

And then comes the best part of all. What does Campbell do? He jumps up and wraps his arms around my neck. This response is perhaps the greatest encouragement I have that we are doing well in this process. Never have I had my children hide from me when facing a spanking. They have never twisted and contorted their bodies to avoid the contact. They have never hid the implements we use for this process. And each time, they look for and receive that reassuring hug from Mom or Dad. As Campbell clings to me he says, "I'm sorry Daddy." And I say, "Campbell, Daddy forgives you, and Daddy loves you. Daddy loved you before you fell into this sin. Daddy loved you in the midst of punishing you. And Daddy will love you all the days of your life, no matter what." And I hold him and I hold him and I hold him, as he squeezes me so hard. Soon his tears begin to dry up as I hold him and remind him that it's all over now.

Campbell stands up, and is ready to go back out to play. But I am not finished. I often, but not every time, look him in the eye and ask him, "Son, what is God's promise?" He replies, "If we confess our sins He is faithful and just to forgive us our sins and to cleanse us from all unrighteousness" (1 John 1:9). The amazing thing though is that so often, as he is reciting this passage, both his eyes and mine begin to well up again. Father and son, in the context of this discipline, have an occasion to be overwhelmed by the grace of God. We enjoy a gospel party. "Isn't it grand, son? Isn't it glorious?" I'll ask him.

If the occasion for which I discipline my son is a recurring weakness (and thankfully, shoving his sisters is not a recurring weakness) I often also find myself dealing with discouragement. This, to a point, is a good thing. We want our children to aspire to godliness. We want them to have godly sorrow for their sin. But we want them also to rejoice in gospel promise. God has promised not only to forgive us, but to cleanse us from all unrighteousness. When the children express that discouragement, it is my habit once again to remind them that we are in this together, that Daddy has recurring sin issues that he needs to deal with. I am not a sinless man trying to drag my children up to my level of spiritual maturity. I am a sinner saved by grace, and called to lead my family into a life of repentance and spiritual growth.

We finish our discipline with a prayer. Campbell remembers to pray these three things. First, he asks that God would forgive him for his sin. Second, he thanks God that His Son died on the cross and that his sins are forgiven. Third, Campbell asks God that He would help him to grow in grace, to be more obedient. Please note, by the way, that such a prayer isn't just for children. It is the appropriate response when anyone sins. Please, when you sin against your children, and you do and will, be certain not only to repent, but to pray this prayer with them. It will teach them a potent lesson, which is a good thing, and will humble you, which is a great thing.

The last injunction I will give my son at this point is to remind him that he needs to go and repent to his sister as well. He must look her in the eye, and speak with sincerity, his desire to have her forgive him. She too has a very specific response. In our family we do not respond to, "Please forgive me" with "That's okay" or "Don't worry about it." We respond instead with, "I forgive you." At this point the relationship is restored. Peace prevails in our home. Grudges are banished, and we move from grace to grace.

We provoke our children to wrath when we punish them in our anger, when we punish them retributively. We likewise provoke our children to wrath when we fail to discipline them, because we want to be their buddy. I love my children, all of them. I delight to spend time with them, and am counting the words as I write so that I can go and be with them. We play together and have great fun together. We laugh together with great joy. But I am always Daddy. I am always the authority in our home (and my authority backs up the authority of my dear wife). I am the head of my home, and my children are always conscious of that, and in fact are comforted by it. Your children don't want you to be their buddy. They have buddies. Instead they look to you for protection, not only from others, not only from brothers who shove them, but from themselves. They want you to drive folly far from them. They want to know that you're there to protect them from themselves.

Do you love your children? Do you want it to go well with them on the earth? The world tells us that the path to the good life lies in getting a great education, acquiring skills that the market values, and making a great living. God's Word tells us that the path to the good life is learning to honor our father and our mother. And it calls fathers and mothers to teach their children to do just that. How then do we do this? We exercise our authority in the exercise of discipline. We do not provoke our children to wrath, but bring them up in the training and admonition of the Lord. We teach them who they are, and we help them to be what they are called to be. We teach them to put *their* trust in the true and living God, and we do this simply enough, by putting *our* trust in the true and living God. There is no perfect formula. You cannot mix together a dash of this kind of discipline with a smattering of that wisdom from some child-rearing guru, mix it together and bring forth model children. Instead you must strive to be faithful. Trust God's Word and cry out for His mercy. We are the tools in His hands.

As you face this daunting task, remember this as well. How much does your heavenly Father love you? He allows you to be called His child. And the Lord chastens those whom He loves. Trust Him, and your children will learn to trust you. Welcome His chastening hand, and they will welcome yours. Delight in His love for you, and they will delight in your love for them. By His grace, in the end they will rise up and call you blessed. For blessed you will be. He has so promised. And our Father always speaks the truth.

Chapter Eight:
Questions and Answers

In this last chapter, my father and I have a dialogue about homeschooling, which my wife and I have found to be a great tool and gift from the Lord, and is a crucial part of our family's identity. In the process, we discuss key issues of family life and God's design for our families.

R.C. Sproul, Senior: One of the main questions to come out of your talks has to do with the phenomenon that I never, in my wildest dreams, could ever have imagined would take place in the United States of America, and that's the homeschooling movement, where literally millions of children have been taken out of the public school system by their parents, or even out of the Christian school system. These parents have taken upon themselves the responsibility of teaching their children at home. And I know that you and Denise are involved in this enterprise of homeschooling, and I'd like to know is this something you prefer to do as a personal preference, or do you recommend this for other people?

R.C. Sproul, Junior: Well, I would probably answer in the latter to that. It is something that I recommend, in fact, it's not at all unusual for me to speak at homeschooling conferences and things such as that. I recognize that different families are in different circumstances and different situations and affirm that there might be, in some circumstances, better choices for other particular families. The benefits of homeschooling are, to my mind, just astounding. You not only have, of course, the freedom and the duty to instill in your children all that we've been talking about—to raise them in the culture of God, and remembering that everything that we teach is taught in the context of the authority of God and the authority of God's Word. We not only have prayer, we not only can read the Bible, we not only can meet at the pole, so to speak, but every moment of every day when we're teaching our children, we're teaching them the context of all truth belonging and coming from the one true God, the God of the Bible, which is something you can't do in the public school system.

Senior: Do you think there's such a thing as a neutral educational curriculum?

Junior: Absolutely not. It depends on what you mean by neutral. If you mean by neutral, "true," yes, it's the Christian way of doing things. We have this tendency to think that if we teach our children the Christian faith or teach them whatever we're teaching them in the context of the authority of God, that somehow we're not being fair.

Senior: Or we're not being really academically honest.

Junior: Right.

Senior: That we're not being disassociated and detached from the evidence. We convince ourselves that we're actually propagandizing our children or inculcating them in a religious viewpoint, whereas the public school doesn't do that.

Junior: Right. And of course everybody does come from a particular point of view—in the public school, in the home school, in the Christian school—and what we're doing, what we're saying, is that we believe this is true. This is why we do this.

Senior: In other words, if you teach mathematics from a perspective of the sovereignty of God, that's one perspective. But if you said, "Well God has nothing to do with mathematics," that's a different perspective. But it's actually a theological position.

Junior: Exactly. It's religious. You know I had the opportunity several years ago to participate in a panel discussion at a conference on the issue of the relationship of children and public schools. One of the men on the panel , Bill Spady, who's known as the father of outcome-based education was given the task of trying to persuade the Christians in the audience that their children were safe in public schools. He argued, "If you come to the public school, we're not interested in undoing your children's convictions—that outcome-based education is all about choices, and we want to lay down choices. We don't want to say, 'No,' to any point of view in outcome-based education. That's why your children are safe with us."

Now my job was to respond to his talk, and I stood up, and I said, "I'm a Christian. I'm a reformed Christian. I'm a Presbyterian, reformed Christian. I'm a reformed, Presbyterian, postmillennial Christian." I went on and added about thirty qualifiers about my convictions, and then I said, "Every morning when I wake up, my job is to teach my children all of those things, and every night when I go to bed, I pray that they will learn these things because the reason I am all these things is because I believe all these things to be true. So don't tell me you want to give my children choices. My job is not to give my children choices. My job is to teach my children the truth, and homeschooling, more than any other option—I recognize in that long list that there are Christians who don't share all those convictions that are my brothers and sisters in Christ, that I am to love and all that—but when I have my homeschool, I get to give what I believe."

Senior: And this outcome-based business is really a thinly-veiled form of relativism.

Junior: It's not even veiled, that's how thin it is. So I think homeschooling is the ideal choice. I think that, again, there are circumstances where people might be in a situation where they would be better off in a Christian school, and I understand that when I teach my children, I never teach them with just me. The second I hand my child a book, I'm now bringing into the equation other views, unless it's one of my books. And understand that I don't want to draw some hard and fast line. In fact, one of the things that I do is teach homeschooled high schoolers. I invite them to gather together. We have a little academy that meets once a week, and I teach a few classes. I'm not against that, and because I'm not against that I don't want to say, "No, you can't go to Christian school." But I do think the more control and authority you have over the rearing of your own children, the better off you are.

Senior: Well, you know quite well that before we even began Ligonier Ministries over thirty years ago, that I had a personal friendship with Francis Schaeffer, and in fact I had several consultations with him regarding the founding of Ligonier Ministries and we carried on a personal friendship until the time that he died. And about twenty years ago, he and I were both sharing a platform at a theological seminary where we were both speaking, and we met each other at the airport in that particular city and shared a cab ride from the airport to our hotel. And I remember that particular encounter with Fran because I asked him on the way, "What is your greatest concern right now to the Christian community in the United

States?" He did not hesitate. His immediate response was, "Statism." And what he meant by statism—not that we simply have a government and a free government, even a good government, and we're patriotic and loyal and all of that stuff—but he was concerned with the word "state" with that three letters put on the end of it—"ism." When it becomes an ideology where our meaning and existence is defined in terms of the state.

Junior: Which is more than ideology. It's a religion.

Senior: Yes, and I've noticed a subtle change in nomenclature—maybe not so subtle—in the last decade or so, where we used to customarily describe the secular educational systems as public education—the public school system, which was a part of the fabric of American tradition. But in the last ten years, you hear it more as "government schools" because there's been a much greater centralization, a much greater involvement in curriculum planning and the government of the school system by the secular state, and we've seen a growing hostility towards anything Christian included in that realm. And again, what Schaeffer was saying to me was not his biggest concern for America as a nation being statism. His biggest concern was for the church in American being statism. And I've just often wondered what he would say if he were here today to see his concerns come to fruition, and I think that that's part of the response of the homeschool movement, that Christian parents are saying, "This far, no further. We're going to take control. We're going to recover our children."

Junior: Well, when we ask the state, or even permit the state to educate our children, we're already—even if they loved the Christian faith—we're already guilty of responsibility drift. God has given parents this obligation. Now again, there may be a degree to which we can delegate this to someone outside the home...

Senior: *In loco parentis.*

Junior: But you can't delegate it to a whole different alien institution like the state, because all education is inherently religious.

Senior: You know a few years ago I did a series of lectures in states that had just come out of the Iron Curtain environment. I was in what was then Czechoslovakia. I lectured for a week in Prague, and then I went to Budapest for a week of lectures, and then on to Romania. And this was very shortly after the great breakdown of the Soviet Union. What I most remember about that trip were conversations I had with Christians in Hungary, as I was asking them about the Hungarian Revolution in the fifties and the Russian tanks and the kids with the stones and all of that, and they were telling me horror stories. They were telling me that the school set up a kind of a system, and required the children to tell the school officials if their parents tried to pray with them at home. And they—the Christian parents—still did. They continued to pray, and they had to sit and tell their six-year-old, "You must not tell this to your school teachers, because we could go to jail or we could be killed." I just couldn't imagine that that could happen in the world in our day, and I guess that's how naïve I am. But people need to really be careful about that.

But here's a question with respect to homeschooling, a common question, I think. I'm sure you've heard it many times. "Some say that homeschooling is the most biblical way of teaching children, however, in this environment, homeschooled children are, to a certain degree, isolated from other children, from their culture, and so on. How do you prepare children who are, in a sense, sheltered from the world with the homeschool experience? How do you prepare them to be salt and light? How do you prepare them to function in a strange and foreign land?"

Junior: Well you know that is a gracious way of asking the question. A lot of times when people are unhappy with the idea of homeschooling, they drop this accusation: "You're sheltering your children," and I have a prepackaged response to that. "What are you going to accuse me of next, feeding and clothing them?"

I think that this is a happy and a healthy thing, keeping our children distinct from the world around them. Our problem in the church is that we think the way to be salt is to be rotten meat and the way to be light is to be darkness. We want our children to be distinct, to be a city on a hill, not a light hidden under a bushel.

Now my children right now, we interact with people outside of our family. In fact another way of expressing that problem is the "socialization problem," which is the number one objection to homeschooling. And I've got another answer for that. "You're concerned about socialization?" And they say, "Yes," and I say, "And you think that means the ability to get along with people who are different?" And they say, "Well, yeah. That's a good summary." And I say, "So your solution is to lock my child in a room with kids exactly their age all day long?" My children interact all day long with their younger brothers and sisters, their older brothers and sisters, their mommy and daddy and people who come into our home. And when we go out into the world, and we do, with all manner of grown-ups, and the grown-ups can't believe it when I take my children to the grocery store. Right now we're in a place politically where I don't have to homeschool in a catacomb. I can tell people, "Yes, we homeschool our kids," and I'll tell them, "Go ahead and ask them something. Ask them the capitols of their states." "The capitol of Virginia is Richmond." The kids just rattle off a little of what they've learned and some people can't believe it.

We have another experience like that when we go out to eat. We go out there into restaurants where there's actually unbelievers.

Senior: No.

Junior: Yes it's true, and when we unload out of the van, you can see all the staff in the restaurant just have this look of dread and panic, when we start strolling in with all these kids. They're terrified. And when we're walking out having eaten, they're slapping us on the back saying, "I can't believe this! What are you guys doing?" And we are light for the world. We say, "Look, we're showing the world that children are, in fact, a blessing." Children can be raised in the nurture and admonition of the Lord. Children can be obedient and pleasant and can have a conversation with a grown-up. And we want them to be able to do that.

Now in terms of preparing them for going out, they're already going out, and they're going out understanding that there is a difference between us and them. There's something in common—we're all sinners—but there's a difference in that we serve King Jesus.

Senior: Let me ask you this. We have an audience here that we always have here at Ligonier when we tape our programs, and I kid with our audience—I call this God's waiting room because the vast majority of people who come are long retired, and they're up in years and we have a great time. But not everybody in this class is in that category. We have my best student right up here in the front row—Roger. How old are you, Roger?

Roger: Thirteen.

Senior: And how long have you been coming to these tapings—three or four years?

Roger: Yes, sir.

Senior: Okay, since before his feet could hit the ground. And Roger is homeschooled, and part of his homeschool curriculum is to come to these tapings, and I think that he gets along great with the people in our classroom. He's a part of this classroom, and I don't think he's suffering socially.

Junior: No, I don't think so either.

Senior: All right, but here's the next question. I'm sure you've also heard it many times. Homeschool or Christian schools? Certainly homeschool requires a tremendous amount of commitment in terms of time and energy, but it also has an economic impact because it requires somebody to be home. You can't have both the mother and father working all day. And add to that the single mother who can't homeschool because she has to go out and earn money to support her child. What do you say to people like this, where there's tremendous economic pressure?

Junior: Well, I want to be careful and gracious, but I think to answer the question you have to go back further. And this is one of the things that I believe about homeschooling that I even want homeschoolers to grasp—and many of them haven't yet. When I go to speak at a homeschooling conference, they often ask me, "How many children do you have?" "Six." "And what are their ages?" "Nine, seven, five, four, two, and one." "So you only have two or three in your homeschool?" And I'll say, "No, I have six in my homeschool. All of my children are in the homeschool because we're always teaching all of them."

Now in the lecture on the church and the family I talked about how our church had a widow who had two small children, and one of the reasons we took care of her needs is because she had a homeschool with her four-year-old and her two-year-old, because she had to teach them. So one of the answers, basically, is for the family to take care of these needs, and then if they can't, for the church to take care of these needs. When it comes to education I'm so committed to not having our families choose the option of having the state educate their children that I want to be like Mother Theresa, who said on the abortion issue on unwanted children, "Send them to us." If you can't educate your children, move to Virginia. I'll teach your children, and I won't charge you anything because that's how important this is, and I'd love to see churches recognize this, pick up that slack, and do what God's called them to do.

Now some of the folks who cry, "Poor," really aren't. It is a sacrifice, and you certainly will have more stuff with two incomes than you will with one income. The same is true for my family.

Senior: Your wife's a certified schoolteacher, and she gave up her job to stay home and teach your kids.

Junior: Right, and I'm delighted she did that and that I can be involved as well. What a great reward it is—not just in the terms of the future of my children, but in terms of the peace of our house and the joy in our house.

Senior: You talk about cultural ideals and the ways of the world. In our culture we're taught from day one that anything more than two children is a burden, and yet, biblically, the more children we have the more the blessing.

Junior: Right, children are a blessing.

Senior: And people have argued, "Well that was in an agrarian culture, and so on, but now in today's industrialized world..." Again, economically more than two children is the worst curse that could befall a family. And when I see how important my family is to me—I mean we only have two children: you and your sister; but Vesta had four miscarriages, and we would have been absolutely delighted to have had six, because the older I get, the more important to me my children are.

Junior: Of course.

Senior: And there are lots of things that I enjoy in this world. I enjoy my house, but I wouldn't trade ten houses for one of my children.

Junior: No, of course not, and the house is going to crumble and become rubble one day.

Senior: That's right.

Junior: Children last forever.

Senior: And it's a value thing, isn't it.

Junior: Yeah. Let me add one more thing on how these things all relate. This is a fascinating study going back to the issue of statism. One of the ways that we solve this problem is by solving other problems because they're all related. If you were to go and draw a chart of the average income brought into the family economy by working wives, starting back forty years ago, and you were to chart the growth of that—income brought in by wives. And if you were to go back and draw another chart of the increase in the tax burden on the family starting forty years ago and chart that, you would think you had drawn only one chart. They are absolutely right on track with each other.

Senior: Say that again.

Junior: The growth of the income by having the wife work has grown at exactly the same rate and is exactly the same number...

Senior: The same amount of money.

Junior: ...as the growth of the tax burden on the family, which means this: Our wives are going out to work to serve the state.

Senior: Well, R.C, again, I wish every Christian parent in America could listen to this series. I was instructed by it, and it's a delight for me to be instructed by my own son. And again, I wish that I would have known when you were a little tyke what you've taught me since. Although, I don't think that it's your desire—it's certainly not mine—to put a guilt trip on anybody.

Junior: No.

Senior: That's not the point. But, I think we need to be encouraged to know that being parents in a godly home can turn the world upside down and that God has given us a mission field and a platform for influencing this world for the kingdom's sake.

Junior: It is an incredible opportunity. It is God's engine for building His kingdom.

Senior: Some of the folks in our audience wanted to know if you could take a moment to clarify the meaning of the term "covenant," since throughout your lectures, you talked about the covenant family, the covenant of redemption, the relationship to the church is a covenant, and so on. Can you just give us a little bit of explanation about that?

Junior: I can try to give a little bit of explanation about it. But covenant, as I said, is so central and so important to our understanding of all of the Bible and our relationships, that it's very difficult to narrow it down, to answer it quickly. But, basically, the covenant is a series of obligations, that when God comes to man and says, "This is what I want you to do. This is what you're required to do. And I'm going to agree to do this." When He makes all of the promises He makes to Abraham or when He even speaks to Adam and Eve in the garden, there's a series of agreements. And then, included with that, are sanctions for obedience or disobedience.

Senior: Let me interrupt you. You say, first of all, there are obligations.

Junior: Yes.

Senior: And then you said promises.

Junior: Yes. Because God promises to do particular parts.

Senior: Oh. All right. Now, when God promises to do something...

Junior: It's an obligation.

Senior: Well, was He obligated to promise it in the first place?

Junior: No, absolutely not. One of the things that we emphasized in this series is that what we miss about covenant when we look at it in terms of contract is that it's not negotiated. When God comes and essentially, makes this deal, one, the very fact that He makes the deal is because of grace.

Senior: Right.

Junior: And second, the fact that if we obey and He blesses us is absolute grace. I mean, broader grace. So, it's always gracious. God doesn't have an obligation to promise to do something for us.

Senior: But once He makes the promise...

Junior: He does have an obligation based on His own character.

Senior: ...on His integrity.

Junior: Right.

Senior: And that's the basis of our whole relationship with Him.

Junior: Absolutely.

Senior: Because we have a God who's made promises to us that we don't deserve.

Junior: That's right.

Senior: But once He makes those promises, He keeps His word.

Junior: Yes, He does.

Senior: And we're supposed to reflect that in our own relationships.

Junior: Absolutely. And keep our word and be in obedience to Him in all the obligations that He gives us, not only in our relationship to Him, but in our obligations with each other. That's what we've talked about—husbands and wives and children—they have obligations amongst each other.

Senior: So, we have a covenant with God.

Junior: Right.

Senior: But, we also have covenants with each other.

Junior: Which is a part of our covenant with God, because God gives us the covenants with each other.

Senior: Okay. So, you said, a moment ago—when I interrupted—you said there are obligations, there are promises, there's an agreement here between two or more parties.

Junior: Right.

Senior: But, you also said covenants have sanctions. Now, what do you mean by sanctions?

Junior: Well, when we talked about sanctions, God comes and says, "If you keep my covenant, here are all manner of blessings that I will bestow upon you." In fact, if you want to reduce God's covenants with man down to their bottom line, it's this: "Obey me and be blessed. Disobey me, and be cursed."

Senior: And those are the exact words that the Old Testament writer, in Deuteronomy, uses: blessing and curse. And our whole understanding of the cross is based on that, isn't it?

Junior: Right. In fact, the cross is, in a sense, almost an addendum to this fundamental covenant that we disobeyed. But Jesus is instead cursed and bears the cross that we deserve.

Senior: That's because He takes, on the cross, Jesus receives the negative covenant sanction of His people who have disobeyed God.

Junior: Right.

Senior: So, we even understand the cross in terms of the covenant.

Junior: Right. But, in His life of total obedience, He earns the blessings. And that is also imputed to us, and so we receive His blessings. The wonderful thing about the Gospel is that it doesn't undo this fundamental covenant, but rather, fulfills it, fits within it, such that God is both just and justifier. God keeps His promise, in terms of His own integrity, by sending the curse on Jesus and by granting us the rewards.

Senior: You just quoted the Apostle Paul in Romans 3, where Paul says—when he's talking about our redemption in the gospel—that God is both "just and the justifier." You know what, R.C.? I think that if we really understood that one sentence—that God is both just and justifier—it would have a profound impact on our understanding of the whole scope of the Christian faith.

Junior: Absolutely.

Senior: Now, here's another question that came from our audience. How does this covenant family series that we've just listened to with your lectures apply to grandparents?

Junior: Well, in another book called *Family Practice*, I have a chapter that I wrote entitled, "A Thirty-Year-Old Child," in which I addressed this. I asked the question, "What is the obligation of a grown child toward their parents?" And I talked about how parents, older parents who have older children, have a role to fulfill of leadership. If you look in Scripture, what you see as God's covenant expands, you see that God makes covenant with Adam and Eve, with these two people. Then, as we move forward, He makes covenant with Noah. We've got Noah and his wife, his three sons and their wives. And then, He makes covenant with Abraham and Abraham has become a clan. If you remember when he goes out to rescue Lot, there's quite a few people there to help him. He's become this little clan and Abraham serves as the patriarch of that clan. And, of course, later, so does his son, Isaac. And it moves forward that way until finally it becomes a nation.

Well, what I would like to see, and what I think the Scripture presents for us, is an image for older men and women who have children, which become grandparents, is that they serve in that role of the patriarch and the matriarch. And that function is this: Their duty is to maintain a kind of consistency and obedience in the broader family while recognizing the absolute authority of the husband over the local family. So, it becomes a sort of advisory role. And that means that I, as a grown man with my own family, have a duty. When I need counsel to whom do I go? I go to you, which I'm sure a lot of other people would like to be able to do. I go to you because you are the patriarch of the clan. But if you say, "R.C., you must buy this house and sell that house," I have the authority and the freedom to say, "Thank you for your counsel, but I'm not going to do that."

Senior: Wait, wait, wait, wait. What?

Junior: I will weigh it, and I need to weigh it—take it very seriously, and speak to you. Look at it this way. Remember in our talk on the children about the two verses that I teach my children. "Children obey your parents in the Lord" and "Honor your father and your mother." Now, these two words "honor" and "obey" are very related. And I have a duty, as long as I'm under your covenantal authority, before I establish my own authority as a man, I have a duty to obey. When that ends, I continue to have the duty to honor. Now, I want to say something else I didn't get a chance to say about that. As we're working in our families—trying to affirm these covenants and to honor our parents—one of the things that parents need to do to help their children learn to honor and obey them is watch carefully how they speak about their own parents. Children will reflect the model that their parents have. And if my children see me speak respectfully and honorably about you and your wife, my mother, then they're going to learn this is part of what this means. And that is passed on, and they're going to learn more powerfully to honor and respect me and my wife, your daughter-in-law.

Senior: Okay then, I have a little different question, but related to this. Somebody raised what I thought was a poignant question today, and it is this: "When I was a young, married person and rearing our children, my wife and I weren't Christians. We didn't become Christians until after our kids were grown. So we did not raise our children in a Christian home. We did not raise them in the nurture and admonition of the Lord. And now our children are grown. Now what?"

Junior: Well, I think that brings to mind a bit of wisdom that a pastor, who lives near me, gave me one time. He was asked a very complicated question, and his answer was, "Sin complicates things." That is poignant. It is heartbreaking. It's almost like the situation that Paul deals with when you have a grown man and a grown woman, they're married and one of them, the wife, becomes a believer and her husband doesn't. And what does Paul say to do? Paul says, "Obey your husband. Submit to him as much as you can. Don't harass him. Don't fuss at him. And maybe, in God's providence and in God's grace, that might win him." So, what parents who become Christians later in life want to do is the same thing they want to do with other unrelated unbelievers. They want to model and reflect the godly, biblical life. They want to tell their children the Gospel. Tell their children, "This is what's happened to us." And pray that God would, through their example, lead these children into the kingdom.

Senior: Now, one of the words that I'm interested in, and maybe, if I can frame this question, I'll be, sort of, addressing it myself. But one of the things that we're interested in are family traditions. I detect, in the culture in which we live today, a growing antipathy towards tradition and traditionalism. We are very much a popular culture that lives for the moment, in the here and now, and tend to despise outmoded traditions. We've seen *Fiddler On the Roof* and what happens when traditions crumble and decay, and so on. And we also know that in biblical terms, Jesus was strongly critical of the scribes and Pharisees because they replaced the Word of God with the traditions of men. And so, many Christians, therefore, infer that the traditions are bad. And yet, in the New Testament, Paul speaks about the *paradosis*, that which has been given over, that which he received from the Lord, which is what we call the Apostolic Tradition. There is a tradition that has its roots and basis in God.

Junior: That's right.

Senior: And it's that tradition that you are talking about with the *shema*, that parents have the responsibility to instruct their children in the divine tradition.

Junior: Right.

Senior: Now, how do you do that? And what kind of traditions do you have in your house that reinforce the divine tradition?

Junior: Well, I think that one of our bad traditions, in terms of time, in America is that we have this vision of child-rearing that is, in essence, consumeristic. That is, that there are too many parents out there who think that my job, as a parent, is to lay before my children all the options there are, and hope and pray that they choose the right one, which is the exact opposite of what the *shema* teaches and what Paul teaches in Ephesians 6. We're not called, as parents, to lay out these choices before our children; we are to put them on this path and lay this path down for them. And traditions are a part of doing that.

Now, you know, what kind of practical traditions can you do? I think that one thing we do in our family—you might call it a tradition or you might call it a good habit— but we practice family worship in our home. And, in one sense, it's not a complicated thing, but it's a little bit too involved to get into a deep explanation of what we do. It involves memorizing Scripture, it involves memorizing the Westminster Shorter Catechism, which is our tradition. We're Presbyterian, but it's our tradition because we believe it's what the Bible teaches. We do singing and praying, and we open the Word and I give little thirty-second sermons after every little passage that I read. And what I'm teaching my children, and I want to be careful that we don't turn family worship into a means to an end. You know, the first question of the Shorter Catechism is, "What is the chief end of man?" The chief end of man is to glorify God and to enjoy Him forever. When we're gathered together as a family for family worship, that's what we're there for. So, whatever comes out of it is just icing. And that includes things like, again, helping them understand their identity. This is what we are. We are worshippers. We're not people who go out and do our own thing six days a week and for one hour on Sunday morning we become this other thing. But, this is what we always are. And, of course, in the teaching that we are instilling in them, what it is that we affirm, what it is that we believe. It teaches them, also, in a wonderful way, what we sing. And I have a friend who teaches on worship, and he says, "You know, we think that what children want to do is to learn children's songs: "Jesus Loves Me," "B-I-B-L-E," and all that because they love that. And you know why they love that? Because that's what we teach them. Instead, if we teach them the hymns of the faith, they'll love those."

We have a video of Darby, my oldest, when she's four and she's in bed. Denise videotaped her bedroom door because we didn't want to go in and disturb her. She's lying in bed singing "Holy, Holy, Holy" or "A Mighty Fortress Is Our God" or "Amazing Grace" just for fun because this is what she's learned. And, again, that places her in a tradition or in a covenant community that's broader than even our family. We're a part of the church of Jesus Christ and this is what we do. So, there's a lot of things that you can do in instilling in them this vision of what they are. We've talked so much about demographics, that their identity is not only not their particular age or gender or whatever. Their identity is part of this family. But it's bigger than that, too. Their identity is that they're part of the church of Jesus Christ.

Senior: R.C., I don't want to put you on the hot seat here and create a controversy for you...

Junior: But, you will.

Senior: Yeah. But, I'm going to because one of the most important and richest traditions that we have in the church is the celebration of the Lord's Supper. And I know that in our tradition, our theological and ecclesiastical tradition, the majority report is opposed to paedo-communion, that is, including children at the Lord's table. And there's a whole case for that as you're aware. But there's also a minority report, in reformed theology that favors paedo-communion. And you stand in the minority group, I think.

Junior: Yes, I do.

Senior: Without giving a defense of that, apart from that whole dispute, isn't it also important for us to help introduce our children to the broader traditions of the church?

Junior: Yes. And one of the ways that we do—and this might be a more controversial thing—one of the ways that we do that in our family and in our church is our children are in church with us, that we come together as families into the sanctuary of God, and we worship together as families. And that, again, tells them that it's not your demographic that goes down the hall to go do this, but, rather, we're going to worship together as families, and that's a part of your identity. And we want you to participate and it's not a burden, for goodness sakes. It's a joyful thing. I love it when we have visitors in our church and when we stand up to sing a song and I'm in the pulpit and I look up and I see their eyes get like saucers. They turn around because they've heard my little children and the other little children, three and four years old, belting out the songs, singing with us, together, the Apostles' Creed, or the Nicene Creed, or reciting together the liturgy of our church. And they can't believe it. But, this is what our children are. We're a part of this broader thing and when we come to the table, whether our children can eat or not, when we come to the table at the Lord's Supper, we teach them, and in our church, we teach the children and the adults that here we're not just us, but all of God's people are together. We're all of God's people gathered around Christ's throne. We're all there as one body. My children know that you're here, right now, with Martin Luther. You're here, right now, with John Calvin. You're here, right now, with Father Abraham. All of us are gathered together. It's like coming and there's your great-great-great-great grandfather at the table. And you're, by the way, you're here with your great grandfather, your father, and we're all here together. And that, again, gives them this vision, this identity, of what they are.

Senior: That whole concept, you know, like you mentioned about the four sections of individual, and the family, and the church, and state, and so on, that we are, perhaps, one of the most individualistic cultures in the history of the world. And it's utterly foreign to the biblical culture. The biblical culture has a principle of corporate solidarity that's completely foreign to the culture in which we live here today. So that, when the Philippian jailer says, "What must I do to be saved?" Paul says, "Believe in the Lord Jesus Christ, and you and your whole household..."

Junior: Right.

Senior: And he assumed that this was not an individualistic experience for the jailer.

Junior: God makes covenants with families.

Senior: Well, let me ask you the next question. What books or programs do you recommend, what helps are there? A lot of people say, "I want to raise my children in a godly home. I want to be a godly parent. I want to take these responsibilities. I feel guilty that I don't do more than I do, but the truth be told, I don't know how." How can you teach me? What kind of literature or help can you give me?

Junior: There's a lot of outstanding materials out there, like there haven't been in ages. And that's one of the things that's exciting about the age we live in, that what happens is that as the culture gets nastier and nastier and gets distinct from the church, more and more people begin to say, "Well, no, we can't do that." And they go back to the Scriptures and they say, "What are we called to do?" And God has raised up so many godly teachers, in our age, to do just that. There are wonderful books out there by Douglas Wilson. He's done a whole series of books on the family. And his wife, Nancy Wilson, has written two books for wives: *The Fruit of Her Hands* and *Praise Her In* *the Gates*, both are good books. Doug has written a book on childrearing called, *Standing On the Promises* that's very much along the lines of what we're talking about. He's got a book on marriage called *Reforming Marriage*. He even has written a wonderful book on courtship, which is something that the church is beginning to recover from her history, that looks at the marrying of our children in a more covenantal, familial way, it's called *Her Hand In Marriage*. Now, there are other wonderful men and teachers out there, on childrearing and discipline. People like Ted Tripp and his brother Paul, have both written good books. *Age of Opportunity* is one of them. *Shepherding a Child's Heart* is another really good one. There are also very good materials out there for family worship, the best of which, I think, is *Tabletalk* magazine. You know, just a few years ago we made what on one hand was a very small change, but on the other, a very large one, when the page that introduces the daily Bible studies began to include a list of some songs for families to sing together, some catechism to memorize, so that our readers can do this together as a family. That's great. There's also a wonderful book called, *Family Worship* by my friend, Kerry Ptacek, published by Greenville Press. And that's just a handful of things that are very helpful and that have helped me.

Senior: Well, let me ask you this. When spiritual leadership rests on the father and there's a rebellious teenage child in the home of a minister, how should his role in the church be handled? You know, one of the qualifications for elder or for ministers, according to Timothy, is that they rule their own households well. And we saw in the Old

Testament, what happened when Eli failed to discipline his sons, God took them—Eli and his sons—and then when the sons of Aaron offered a strange fire on the altar, God consumed them. Now, how does that influence—let me just also preface this by saying that my daughter, your sister, who's a grown woman, still is very uncomfortable when people say, "You're the minister's daughter." You also know something about this spotlight that's put on ministers' kids. You grew up as a minister's child. What about this?

Junior: Well, I think you want to be careful from focusing the attention on the child because that's not what the passages in Timothy are dealing with. They're dealing with the parent and the parent's obligation. Now, on the issue of what do you do with the pastor with a rebellious teenager, I'm not ready to make a definitive stand on that issue, but I will say this: The vast majority of the evangelical church is way off on this because they completely ignore it. It's an important question. And we need to at least move somewhere towards asking the question. We need to move towards saying, "Okay, now what—obviously something needs to happen here—what is it?" Whether or not that means automatic defrocking, I'm not ready to say. I don't know because I learned from you that these qualifications are general, paradigmatic, that they're the ideal which means that...

Senior: Nobody fulfills all of them perfectly.

Junior: Right. But that doesn't mean that failure to fulfill them is a matter of indifference. And so, I do think it needs to be weighed much more carefully, much more heavily, and it's not just for pastors—what we call teaching elders— it's also for ruling elders. Our tendency in the American evangelical church is to choose ruling elders, principally, on the basis of success in business—prominent people in the community. And that's not on the list.

Senior: But, there are occasions where the parents can be very godly people—do what they're supposed to do—and the child still maintains a rebellious spirit.

Junior: Right.

Senior: But the question is: "Is that rebellion because of a parental negligence or not?" If it *is* a matter of negligence, then that does have bearing upon the qualifications of the person to be in a position of spiritual leadership.

Junior: Which means that we have to have a standard for what looks like negligence and what doesn't look like negligence. And I'm afraid that we're a long way from an appropriate standard. I mean, we think that if the father hasn't completely abdicated, or isn't a drunkard, or doesn't beat the children, then he's a godly father. That's not enough. We need to raise that standard and then apply it in those situations. And I agree that it can happen, that someone can do well. And, by the way, someone who does do well, also fails. No one is the perfect parent. But we need to have some sense of what the standard is and those who don't make it, need to be removed from the office and learn what this means and then, maybe, that changes, I don't know. But I do think it does disqualify somebody.

Senior: Right. Obviously, no one is a perfect parent, I agree with that. Have you ever met anybody that you thought came close to that?

Junior: Absolutely.

Senior: That's what I wanted to hear. But seriously, I do appreciate your responses to these questions because these are questions that many people have. You've touched a raw nerve, not in the sense of creating pain, but you've touched something where we feel that there's something really wrong in the lives of Christians and in the lives of the church. And you've set forth, before us, the distinction between the culture of this world and the culture of God.

POSTSCRIPT

As with so many other biblical truths, our problem isn't so much what we haven't learned, but what we have learned and forgotten. We all know, for instance, that children last forever, while the toys that clutter our lives will all rust. But we still find ourselves hungering for the transient, for the vacuous. This reflects the first frontline of the war we have already written about. The battle between the seed of the woman and the seed of the serpent is most fierce where it is closest to us, in the battle between the old man and the new, between our redeemed nature and our sin nature.

That we often fail in this battle, that we often forget the centrality of our families, is no reason to shirk the battle. Rather it should drive us to gird up our loins like men. There is, however, a decided difference between girding up our loins, and seeking to pick ourselves up by our bootstraps. The difference is in our prayers. A bootstrap mentality is prideful, and ineffective. But the most effective posture for raising and leading a godly family is on our knees.

We are not only to be prophetic to our families, bringing to bear the Word of God on their lives, but we are to be priestly. That is, we are to bring our families before the throne of God. When we who are husbands and fathers feel the weight of our responsibilities, we must cry out to our Father for strength and wisdom. There is no greater power in the work of sanctifying our families than prayer.

In like manner, when we recognize that we have failed, whether it is a brief failure or a lifetime of failure, the Scripture gives us clear direction—we must repent. Over the years as I have taught on the family, I have had people get angry. I have had people express great gratitude. I have had many, particularly among unmarried women and women married to unbelieving or weak husbands, express longing. But nothing touches my heart more than those who respond with regret. Many parents who are past the season in life where they are raising children now recognize that they had failed to see their task in truly biblical terms. And many, with tears in their eyes, concede that they are reaping what they have sown.

Here we especially must remember our ultimate family. We are all together the bride of Christ, who even now intercedes for us before the Father. And we are, in Christ, joint heirs with Him. We have this unspeakable privilege, that He allows us to be called His children. This is why—and the context in which—we repent, each of us, for our failures. None of us is the perfect parent. All of us have missed opportunities. All of us have regrets. And all of us, if we are in Him, have our sins covered.

This is our joy. We have been adopted into the only non-dysfunctional family in the universe. And He who has begun a good work in us has promised to bring us to perfection. If our children are grown, let us pray that He would cover our past failures, and empower us to be godly parents and grandparents. If our children are still with us, then pray that He will empower us to do right by our children. Whatever our circumstances, whether we have just begun the race, whether we ran poorly, or whether we have run well, all of this is in our Father's almighty hands. And so we can be at peace, remembering that Christ never fails. We can be confident that we are indeed, bound for glory.